OLD TESTAMENT GUIDES

General Editor
R.N. Whybray

EZEKIEL

Other titles in this series include

Genesis 1–11 J.W. Rogerson	*Hosea* G.I. Davies
Genesis 12–50 R.W.L. Moberly	*Amos* A.G. Auld
Exodus W. Johnstone	*Jonah and Lamentations* R.B. Salters
Leviticus L.L. Grabbe	*Micah, Nahum, Obadiah* R. Mason
Deuteronomy R.E. Clements	*Zephaniah, Habakkuk, Joel* R. Mason
Judges A.D.H. Mayes	*Haggai, Zechariah, Malachi* R.J. Coggins
1 & 2 Samuel R.P. Gordon	*Joshua* A. Curtis
1 & 2 Chronicles G. Jones	*Isaiah 1–39* J. Barton

Ezra and Nehemiah
H.G.M. Williamson

Job
J.H. Eaton

Psalms
J. Day

Ecclesiastes
R.N. Whybray

The Song of Songs
A. Brenner

Isaiah 56–66
G.I. Emmerson

The Second Isaiah
R.N. Whybray

Jeremiah
R.P. Carroll

Daniel
P.R. Davies

EZEKIEL

Henry McKeating

Sheffield Academic Press

First Published by Sheffield Academic Press 1993
Reprinted 1995

Copyright © 1993, 1995 Sheffield Academic Press

Published by Sheffield Academic Press Ltd
Mansion House
19 Kingfield Road
Sheffield, S11 9AS
England

Printed on acid-free paper in Great Britain
by The Cromwell Press
Melksham, Wiltshire

British Library Cataloguing in Publication Data

A catalogue record for this book is available
from the British Library

ISBN 1-85075-428-4

CONTENTS

Abbreviations   7
Select List of Commentaries   9

1. Introduction   11
2. The Structure of the Book   15
3. Ezekiel the Man   22
4. The History of Ezekiel Criticism: 1900–1950   30
5. The History of Ezekiel Criticism:
    The 1950s to the Present Day   43
6. The Dating Series   62
7. The Theology of Ezekiel   73
8. The Book of Ezekiel and Other Prophetic Traditions   92
9. The Final Vision: Ezekiel 40–48   99
10. Messianism in the Book of Ezekiel   105
11. The nāśî' in Ezekiel   110
12. Gog and Magog: Ezekiel 38–39   114

Index of References   123
Index of Authors   127

125128

ABBREVIATIONS

AB	Anchor Bible
ASTI	*Annual of the Swedish Theological Institute*
ATD	Das Alte Testament Deutsch
BJRL	*Bulletin of the John Rylands University Library of Manchester*
BKAT	Biblischer Kommentar: Altes Testament
BZAW	*Beihefte zur Zeitschrift für die alttestamentliche Wissenschaft*
CBC	Cambridge Bible Commentary on the New English Bible
HSM	Harvard Semitic Monographs
IB	*Interpreter's Bible*
ICC	International Critical Commentary
Int	*Interpretation*
JBL	*Journal of Biblical Literature*
JSOT	*Journal for the Study of the Old Testament*
NCB	New Century Bible
RSV	Revised Standard Version
RV	Revised Version
TBC	Torch Bible Commentaries
TDOT	G.J. Botterweck and H. Ringgren (eds.), *Theological Dictionary of the Old Testament*
TOTC	Tyndale Old Testament Commentaries
VT	*Vetus Testamentum*

Select List of Commentaries

K.W. Carley, *The Book of the Prophet Ezekiel* (CBC; Cambridge: Cambridge University Press, 1974). The Cambridge series prints the NEB text. There is no space for extended or detailed comment. Within the limitations of the series, a valuable commentary.

G.A. Cooke, *The Book of Ezekiel* (ICC; Edinburgh: T. & T. Clark, 1936). A more useful commentary than its date might suggest. Cooke rejected the more radical crititicism of the period in which he wrote. His work is thus more congenial to most current opinion than it was to some of his contemporaries. The strength of the ICC format is that though the reader does not need to be a Hebraist in order to use the commentary, extensive notes on the Hebrew text are additionally provided in smaller print. Few present-day commentaries have full comments on the Hebrew. Cooke predates, of course, the development of form criticism and traditio-historical studies.

W. Eichrodt, *Ezekiel, a Commentary* (ATD; Göttingen: Vandenhoeck & Ruprecht, 1965, 1966; ET: London: SCM Press, 1970). A very important commentary.

S. Fisch, *Ezekiel* (Soncino Bible; Soncino: London, 1950). Contains both Hebrew and English text. The notes are brief but contain material from traditional Jewish commentators not otherwise readily available in English.

M. Greenberg, *Ezekiel* (2 vols.; New York: Doubleday, 1983). A commentary of a different type and with a different approach from any other commentary on Ezekiel. Greenberg opts for what he calls a 'holistic' approach, which means that he deliberately refrains from critical analysis and interprets the text 'as it stands'. See fuller comments below.

H.G. May and E.L. Allen, 'The Book of Ezekiel' (*IB*, VI; New York: Abingdon Press, 1956). *The Interpreter's Bible* not only separates exegesis from exposition, and prints them separately, but allocates them to different commentators. The distinction does not always carry conviction; nevertheless the commentary is not to be neglected.

D.M. Stalker, *Ezekiel* (TBC; London: SCM Press, 1968). The Torch Commentaries are brief and basic, but, within their limiations, helpful.

J.B. Taylor, *Ezekiel* (TOTC; London: Tyndale Press, 1969). Another series of brief and basic commentaries, written from a conservative standpoint.

J.W. Wevers, *Ezekiel* (NCB; London: Nelson, 1969). Fuller than the
  Cambridge Bible but still a manageable commentary, not overburdened
  with detail.

W. Zimmerli, *Ezekiel* (2 vols.; BKAT; Neukirchen–Vluyn: Neukirchener
  Verlag, 1969; ET: Hermeneia; London: SCM Press, 1979). *The* definitive
  large commentary, exploring thoroughly all possible aspects of the
  book, making full use of form-critical and traditio-historical methods.

In addition, commentary on Ezekiel is included, of course, in the various one-
volume commentaries on the Bible. Though these treatments are necessarily
brief, the compressed format seems to concentrate commentators' minds and
the quality of these commentaries is, in general, very high.

J. Muilenburg, 'Ezekiel', in M. Black and H.H. Rowley (eds.), *Peake's
  Commentary on the Bible* (London: Nelson, 1962), pp. 568-90.

W.H. Brownlee, 'The Book of Ezekiel', in C.M. Laymon (ed.), *The Interpreter's
  One Volume Commentary on the Bible* (London: Collins, 1972), pp. 411-
  35.

L. Boadt, 'Ezekiel', in R.E. Brown, J.A. Fitzmyer and R.E. Murphy (eds.), *The
  New Jerome Biblical Commentary* (London: Geoffrey Chapman, 1989),
  pp. 305-28.

F.F. Bruce, 'Ezekiel', in F.F. Bruce, G.D.C. Howley and H.L. Ellison (eds.),
  The International Bible Commentary (Grand Rapids: Zondervan;
  London: Marshall Pickering, rev. edn, 1988), pp. 807-46.

R.R. Wilson, 'Ezekiel', in J.L. Mays (ed.), *Harper's Bible Commentary* (San
  Francisco: Harper, 1988), pp. 652-94.

the land of Israel'. Whether we are meant to understand this as quite the same sort of experience as the one described in ch. 8 is a little hard to decide. In 43.5, still part of the account of the same experience, the prophet is again moved about by the Spirit. Once more, this is not a totally new feature in prophecy, but an old feature which in Ezekiel has been elaborated and made more prominent. 1 Kgs 18.11-12 presupposes that supernatural translocation was something for which Elijah was famous, and 2 Kgs 2.16 confirms this. It is noteworthy that in both texts the agent of translocation is said to be the Spirit of the Lord.

The Spirit of the Lord and the hand of the Lord have been mentioned already in connection with translocation, but they appear throughout the book and are distinctive features of Ezekiel's way of talking about God and how God influences him. The hand of the Lord is mentioned in 1.3; 3.14, 22; 8.1; 37.1 and 40.1. The Spirit is referred to in 2.2; 3.12, 14; 8.3; 11.1, 5, 24; 37.1 and 43.5. It will be noted that some of the same passages appear in both the above lists, illustrating the fact that in Ezekiel the hand of the Lord and the spirit of the Lord are quite strongly associated.

Further Reading

U. Cassuto, 'The Arrangement of the Book of Ezekiel', *Biblical and Oriental Studies* 1 (1973).
S. Talmon and M. Fishbane, 'The Structuring of Biblical Books: Studies in the Book of Ezekiel', *ASTI* 10 (1976), pp. 129-53.

See also the standard textbooks on Introduction to the Old Testament, but especially
W.H. Schmidt, *Introduction to the Old Testament* (London: SCM Press, 1984), pp. 208-14.
R. Rendtorff, *The Old Testament: An Introduction* (London: SCM Press, 1985).
B.S. Childs, *Introduction to the Old Testament as Scripture* (London: SCM Press, 1979).

3

EZEKIEL THE MAN

RARELY, IF EVER, does the Old Testament offer us gratuitous information about the life of a prophet, and certainly never anything that could be called a *curriculum vitae*. Our interest in biography is something which the biblical authors and editors seem not to have shared. Any information that is given about the prophet's personal life is given for a purpose, usually because it is relevant to the prophet's message. It is not given in order to gratify curiosity, and for that reason is generally fragmentary. In what follows, I shall initially take the information that the book offers at something like its face value, and see what kind of picture emerges, though major areas of doubt will be indicated in passing.

In the case of Ezekiel, we do have a number of scraps of information about the prophet's life, but they are no more than scraps. We cannot rely on them to give us a complete picture either of the events of his lifetime or of his character; nor have we any way of knowing whether the picture they do allow us to put together is a balanced one. Many of the scraps of information which we do have come to us in descriptions of various enacted prophecies in which the prophet engaged. They are subservient to the action being performed and its interpretation. We must be sensitive to this fact if we attempt to use them to build up a picture of Ezekiel the man. To take an obvious example, it would clearly be rash in the extreme to use the information that Ezekiel refrained from going into mourning on the death of his wife (24.15ff.) to make any deductions about the prophet's marital relationship.

The scraps of information, therefore, must remain scraps.

1
INTRODUCTION

THE IMPORTANCE OF EZEKIEL can hardly be overstressed. He is placed (assuming that the traditional understanding of his date is correct) at the great crisis point of Israel's history, the exile. The question was, 'Can the nation survive?'

It was a real enough question. Judah's sister kingdom, Northern Israel, had faced a similar experience about a century and a half earlier, and had not survived. That Judah did survive is largely to the credit of the exilic prophets and the nation's other religious leaders.

One form in which the question was put was, 'Can God still be with us?' Ezekiel was one of the people for whom this question was most acute. He seems to have represented the priestly, sacral traditions of Judah, for whom the presence of God *in the temple* was important, and for whom the system of festivals and sacrifices was the heart of religion. How could Judah sustain itself, and any vision of God, or any relationship with him, when deprived of its temple and driven out of the holy city and the holy land, to a place where, according to its own law, no sacrifices were allowable?

The book begins with an assertion that the vision is still possible, even in the land of exile, and the presence still available; and it ends with an elaborate promise of the restoration of the temple and the restitution of God's presence to its place.

For Jeremiah the problem was in some respects less intense. The temple seems to have meant much less to him, and he appears to have been prepared to contemplate the possibility of a religion in which the ark (the ancient symbol of divine presence in the sanctuary) could be cheerfully dispensed with (Jer. 3.16).

The deuteronomic reform some decades earlier had helped both to set up the problem and to prepare for its resolution. It had set up the problem by laying considerable emphasis on the temple, and on the exclusiveness of its worship. Only here, said the reformers, could the festivals rightly be celebrated, and only here could sacrifice be offered. This had the effect of making Judah's religious life very vulnerable to the temple's loss. Without it, what was left that was recognizably the religion of Israel?

But the deuteronomic reform had also recognized that laying such stress on the temple as the only centre of worship held the risk of cutting off many of the people, even within the land of Palestine itself, from regular participation in the means of grace. Deuteronomy therefore stresses the need to develop a domestic piety, centred on the law itself, on which the faithful Israelites are to meditate when they lie down and when they rise up, when they go out and when they come in, and which they should teach diligently to their children (Deut. 6.6-9; 11.18-21).

The book of Ezekiel, though accepting, even asserting, that the people in exile can still know the divine presence and be faithful to the divine will, is building on foundations which Deuteronomy laid; yet neither for Ezekiel nor for the deuteronomists is domestic piety sufficient, and the book of Ezekiel comes to its climax in the restoration of Israel's vital centre, the temple.

Ezekiel's work was vital in his own time in helping Judah to face the trauma and to find its way through it. It is vital in our time to anyone who wishes to understand that crucial episode in the history of the people of God. For it has to be admitted that the book of Ezekiel is not one of the better-known prophetic books. Apart from the description in ch. 37 of the vision of the valley of dry bones, it has no passages which have entered popular consciousness. Many modern readers find both its style and its content uninviting. Much of the book consists of rather wordy discussions (such as ch. 18) or rather fantastical descriptive passages (like the allegory of the great eagle in ch. 17) whose meaning is at first sight far from obvious. Sharp, direct oracles are far fewer here than in other prophets (though they do occur; see, for example 23.32-34; 24.3b-6). And though Ezekiel makes great use of dramatic images, both in the form of visions and of parables (often the same images as are used by his prophetic predecessors), they are developed in new ways. Where earlier prophets are content to sketch in the content of the vision in a rather impressionistic way, or even, without further description, baldly to state the vision's content (a plumb line—Amos 7.8; the rod of an almond tree—Jer. 1.11) Ezekiel will attempt to describe his visions in detail, and develop his parabolic images at length. As to visions, it is instructive to compare Ezek. 1.1–3.15 with Isaiah 6, or with the even terser Amos 9.1. As to parable, compare Hosea 1 and 3 with Ezekiel 16 and 23. To the modern reader it is by no means evident that the greater length of Ezekiel's treatment brings any correspondingly greater clarity. Indeed, one often feels that by comparison with other prophets, Ezekiel by his complexity loses directness and blunts the cutting edge of his imagery.

And yet, the writing does have a power of its own, and certainly an originality. Ezekiel's originality manifests itself both in the *content* of his thought and in the *language* in which it is expressed. In some respects his situation demanded, or at least favoured, the working out of new forms of communication. The exile obliged prophets to make more use of writing. Jeremiah began to do so once the first deportation had taken place (Jer. 29.1-32; 30.1-2). Ezekiel seems to have been the first prophet extensively to commit his own words to writing. (So, at least, many scholars have concluded.) Much of his prophecy, therefore, is likely to have been *conceived* as literary communication from the beginning. This was bound to make a difference to its form.

Furthermore, the book presents Ezekiel as a prophet but describes him in 1.1 as a priest. This is certainly consistent with the kind of materials which the book itself contains, for those seem to draw both on the traditions of the prophetic oracle, prophetic vision, prophetic enactment, and so on, and also on those of priestly decision-making and priestly lawgiving. Ezekiel develops the forms which both prophetic and priestly traditions offered him, and out of them creates something distinctively his own.

Ancient Israel never, as far as we know, produced any drama or developed a theatre, as did the Greeks. Any drama which did take place was probably confined to the liturgy, and the cult may well have satisfied any dramatic urge which Israelites may have felt. It is significant that it is from a cultic background that Ezekiel, the priest, emerges. Perhaps if a dramatic tradition had been available to him Ezekiel would have appeared as a Hebrew Aeschylus or Euripides. His instincts are those of the dramatist. When attempting to convey his message to those around him, his first resort is not the oracle but the prophetic enactment, of which he makes far more use (if our records are any guide) then any of his predecessors. His parables are essentially dramatic, and his visions are pure spectacle. In the descriptions of the visions, and indeed in some of the oracles, the reader is being invited to look in on the theatre that is going on inside the prophet's head. Whether it is the tableau of God enthroned in his glory (ch. 1), the display of the ship of Tyre in its splendour (ch. 27) or the drama of the valley of dry bones (ch. 37), all are essentially spectacular.

2

THE STRUCTURE OF THE BOOK

BEFORE GIVING ANY ACCOUNT of how the book may have taken shape, it is worth looking at what its shape now is. In any scholarly enquiry it is best to begin from what we know, and from what (if anything) is certain. Our reconstructions of the way the book has been shaped are bound to be hypothetical; the structure of the book as it now exists, however, is given, and this must be our starting point.

Several of the prophetic books tend towards a threefold structure, a feature which the book of Ezekiel exemplifies particularly clearly. The scheme begins with oracles of woe against the prophet's own nation, followed by oracles against foreign nations, and these are followed in turn by prophecies of hope and salvation.

In Ezekiel the first section, containing the prophet's message of judgment on Judah and Jerusalem, runs from ch. 1 to ch. 24. Oracles against foreign nations follow in chs. 25–32. The message of salvation and hope is found in chs. 33–48.

The demarcation between the types of material in the different sections is not an altogether rigid one. The first section, of oracles against Judah and Jerusalem, does contain one or two prophecies of restoration, for instance 11.14-21, 16.60-63, 17.22-32. Similarly, though oracles against foreign nations are gathered in the second section, a fairly extensive condemnation of Edom appears outside it in ch. 35. But these exceptions do not invalidate the accuracy of the broad characterization of the sections.

But although the contents of the three sections are clearly distinguished, they are at the same time thematically linked.

This applies especially to sections 1 and 3. In 2.5, following the account of the prophet's call, and at the beginning of the judgment oracles proper, we have the words, 'they will know that there has been a prophet among them'. In 33.33, at the beginning of the salvation oracles, the identical words are echoed. Both sections (1 and 3) present the 'watchman' theme near the beginning (3.16-21 and 33.1-9). The dumbness which is inflicted on the prophet in the call vision (3.25-27), immediately before his prophecies of the destruction of the city, is removed in 33.21-22, when he receives the report of Jerusalem's fall (cf. 24.25-27).

The vision of the divine glory also provides a link. It appears in 1.1ff., at the time of Ezekiel's call, appears again in the account of the visit to Jerusalem in chs. 8–11 (the glory *leaving* the city in 11.22-23), and returns to the temple in 43.1ff.

Less convincingly, the vision of the dry bones in ch. 37 is said to be prefigured in 24.1-14, with its emphasis on the bones. Other, less precise, links and parallels have been pointed out. Those listed above are the clearest ones.

Section 2, the oracles against foreign nations (chs. 25–32), is integrated into the book by its inclusion in the scheme of dates, which runs through all the sections.

Literary and Other Characteristics of the Book of Ezekiel

One of the book's most distinctive features is the particular kind of language which it uses. It is instructive to glance through the larger prophetic books in a translation such as the RSV, which clearly distinguishes poetry from prose by the way they are printed. It will immediately be evident that the book of Isaiah is basically a book of poetry, with a few, mostly brief, prose passage interspersed. Jeremiah is much closer to being equally divided between prose and poetry, though the latter probably still predominates, and the prose occurs in much more extensive slabs. Ezekiel, by contrast, is in substance a prose book, with occasional poetic passages, few of them of any great length.

The book does contain oracular poetry of the kind familiar from other prophetic works, but such material is not prominent. There are occasional brief (and usually rather cryptic) snatches of oracular material, such as 21.9-10 and 24.3b-5. And there are a few more extended poetic passages, mostly amongst the oracles against foreign nations (though ch. 19 is an exception). But the bulk of the book is prose. However, it is not simply the predominance of the prose which is distinctive, but its peculiar quality. It is a rhetorical prose, sometimes rather wordy and repetitive. It is strongly reminiscent of the priestly parts of the Pentateuch, and is full of characteristic and idiosyncratic phrases. Some of the more striking or frequent of these expressions and locutions are as follows:

1. The prophet is often addressed by God as 'son of man'. This occurs nearly one hundred times in the book. This form of address is not used elsewhere in the Old Testament except, in a very different kind of context, in Daniel.

2. God is characteristically addressed, or described, by the double phrase *ᵃdônāy yhwh* (RV and RSV 'Lord GOD', more literally, 'Lord Yahweh'). This double title is not unique to Ezekiel; other prophets use it, but much less often. It occurs, for example, only about a dozen times in Jeremiah, but more than 200 times in Ezekiel.

3. 'Rebellious house' is a phrase applied to the prophet's own people, and is, in this form, peculiar to Ezekiel.

4. 'Behold, I am against...', usually, 'Behold, I am against you'. This is an expression not confined to Ezekiel (it occurs not uncommonly in Jeremiah too) but it *is* typical of him.

5. 'I, Yahweh, have spoken it', sometimes followed by 'and I have done it', or 'and I will do it'. This occurs characteristically as a concluding formula at the end of an oracle.

6. A very characteristic formula of Ezekiel's, also occurring normally at the ends of prophecies, is, 'And they shall know that I am the Lord'.

7. In his prophesying the prophet is on a number of occasions instructed to 'Set your face against...' or 'Set your face towards...'

8. Very characteristic of Ezekiel's style is his habit of introducing a subject by means of a question, usually put into the mouth of God. Chapter 8 provides a series of examples: 8.6, 'Son of man, do you see what they are doing...?'; cf. 8.12, 8.15, 8.17. In addition to all these, there are particular items of vocabulary which Ezekiel prefers. For example, he regularly uses the word *nāśî'* for 'ruler'; of the several available words for 'idols' he favours *gillûlîm*. These word preferences are only really noticeable in the Hebrew, but the peculiar or characteristic turns of phrase are very evident even in translation. All of these points give Ezekiel's prose an unmistakable and recognizable flavour.

Other features of the book will also readily strike the reader. For example, prophetic visions are very prominent in it. Of course, several prophetic books give accounts of visions; there is, for example, a famous series of visions in Amos 7.1-9, 8.1ff. and 9.1ff. But these are fairly typical of the visions in pre-exilic prophetic books in being marked by their brevity. The pair of visions in Jer. 1.11ff. are, if anything, briefer still. Rather more extensive is the description of the vision in Isaiah 6. Yet one only has to set Isaiah 6 alongside Ezekiel's ch. 1 to appreciate that Ezekiel's descriptions belong to quite a different order. The contrast is all the more pointed in that Isaiah 6 and Ezekiel 1 are basically describing exactly the same thing: a vision of the Lord enthroned in glory.

What is distinctive about Ezekiel's descriptions is that they are much more lengthy, more wordy, and seem to be attempting to describe in detail what other prophets are content to refer to baldly and briefly, or at most, to sketch in a rather impressionistic way. The longest and most detailed vision of all is Ezekiel's vision of the restored temple in chs. 40–48.

Furthermore, there is often a rather surreal or fantastic quality about Ezekiel's visions. The vision of the valley of dry bones in ch. 37 has this quality, and so, *par excellence*, has the extraordinary inaugural vision of ch. 1 already referred to. In this matter of surrealism Ezekiel's visions are not without parallel, but such parallels as exist are to be found in post-exilic prophetic texts such as the series in Zech. 1.7–6.8. Alongside the visions go the equally characteristic parables. Indeed, the parable form and the vision form can approximate very closely to one another. The account of the great eagle in ch. 17 is presented as a riddle (*ḥidâ*) and an allegory (*māshāl*) (17.2). But one feels that the same content would have been just as much at home in the company of Ezekiel's visions, and could as readily have been presented in visionary form. The passage has the same surreal quality as have some of the visions.

Other parables, however, are of rather different types. Elsewhere in prophetic literature there is little that could properly be described as 'parable'. At best, we have brief comparisons, little more than similes, although the 'Song of the Vineyard' in Isaiah 5 is an exception, and the parable form is occasionally exemplified in literature outside oracular prophecy, as, for instance, in Judg. 9.7ff. But Ezekiel's parables are extended compositions. The parable of the great eagle has already been mentioned. Perhaps more typical are the parable of the foundling in ch. 16 and that of Oholah and Oholibah in ch. 23. In both of these the prophet tells quite a lengthy story, whose meaning he then goes on to expound. The prophecy against the 'shepherds of Israel' in ch. 34 is also a kind of parable.

The use of visions does have antecedents elsewhere in prophetic literature, and something like the parables are there in embryonic form, but Ezekiel develops each of these genres in idiosyncratic ways. His long arguments and discussions are, however, without antecedents in the other prophetic books. Perhaps the best known of these discussions is the one in ch. 18 about the righteous man who has an unrighteous son and a righteous grandson. More will be said later about these discussions, but for the present it is sufficient to note that their closest parallels are not in other prophetic literature but in priestly law. Their presence in the book certainly contributes to the distinctive impression it makes on the reader.

Very prominent in the book are enacted prophecies, or what Zimmerli calls 'sign-actions'. They make a major contribution to the total effect of the book's peculiar style. Enacted prophecy is a feature apparently endemic in Israelite prophecy from as far back as we can trace it. In the narratives of the early prophets we find a number of examples, of which perhaps the best known is Ahijah's manipulation of the robe in 2 Kgs 11.29ff. In eighth-century prophecy the device is less in evidence, though it never entirely disappears. Isaiah resorts to it in Isaiah 20. And if we regard the giving of symbolic names to children as a kind of enacted prophecy it appears also in Isa. 7.3, 7.14, 8.1-4, as well as Hos. 1.2-9. Hosea's marriage is seen by some interpreters as a kind of enacted prophecy, as, later, Jeremiah's refusal to marry certainly is (Jer. 16.1-4).

In the book of Jeremiah, indeed, enacted prophecy returns to some prominence. Examples are found in Jeremiah 19, 27–28 and 35 and (perhaps even more bizarre than any of those examples) 13.1-11. But Ezekiel makes even more use of the phenomenon than Jeremiah, and some of his enactments seem even more elaborate than Jeremiah's. His miming of the anticipated siege of Jerusalem in ch. 4 is a good example, and (briefer, but perhaps even odder) his cutting off of all his hair at the beginning of ch. 5. Other examples are 12.1-16, 12.17-20, perhaps 21.6-7 (MT 21.11-12), 21.18-20 (MT 21.23-25), 24.15-24 and 37.15-23.

Another disconcerting feature of the book of Ezekiel (disconcerting, that is, to many modern readers) is the frequency with which it speaks of supernatural translocation. The most striking instance of this occurs at the beginning of ch. 8, where Ezekiel is said to have been picked up by the hair of his head by a superhuman being and transported from Babylonia to Jerusalem. In 11.1, while still in Jerusalem, he is lifted up and moved about by the Spirit. And in 11.24 he is reported to have been taken home to Babylonia by the same means. Something similar has already happened in 3.12 and 14, again the agent being the Spirit; compare also 37.1. In 40.1-2 the prophet again pays a visit to Jerusalem, but this time the language employed is rather different. He does not speak directly of translocation, but says that 'the hand of the Lord was upon me, and brought me in the visions of God into

The major historical events through which the prophet lived do, of course, give us a broad framework into which to fit his life. It will therefore be best to deal with the historical background to Ezekiel together with the few known facts about the prophet's life.

The first fall of Jerusalem to the Babylonians took place in 597 BCE and resulted in the first deportation (2 Kgs 24.8-17). When the book of Ezekiel opens the prophet is in Babylon, and the implications of 1.1, 33.21 and 40.1 are that he had been among those first deported.

He appears to have lived at a place called Tel Aviv (3.15), where he had a house (8.1). The exact site of Tel Aviv is not known. It was near what Ezekiel calls 'the River Chebar', which is generally identified with the canal now called Shatt en-nil, which leaves the Euphrates at a point close to Babylon and re-enters it at Uruk.

According to the date given in 1.1-3 Ezekiel received his call to be a prophet near his home in Babylonia on 31st July 593. This is noted in the context of an elaborately described vision of the divine glory, enthroned upon a *merkābâ*, a throne-chariot.

In 1.3 Ezekiel is described as 'Ezekiel the priest'. It is evident from the rest of the book, and from the familiarity which Ezekiel displays with Jerusalem and its temple, that it is the Jerusalem priesthood which Ezekiel represents.

In 1.1 the year 593 (that is, the fifth year after the deportation) is also described enigmatically as 'the thirtieth year'. The meaning of this phrase has been much debated, but it may refer to Ezekiel's age at the time of his call. The reason advanced for this conclusion is as follows. According to Num. 4.23, 30 is the age for taking up priestly/levitical duties (though Num. 8.24 reckons it as 25 years). If we take Num. 4.23 as correct, and 'the thirtieth year' as referring to Ezekiel's age, then the significance of the date would be that Ezekiel's call to prophecy came in the year when he would, if he had remained in Jeruslaem, have embarked on his priestly functions.

The book implies that Ezekiel remained in Babylonia, but in his prophesying directed a good deal of his attention to the Palestinian homeland, the kernel of his message at this period being that further disaster was in store.

In 3.25-27 he claims that shortly after his call he was struck dumb, and that the dumbness was only relieved five years later, when the news came of the second fall of Jerusalem in 586 (33.21-22; cf. 24.27). Much is unclear about this experience of dumbness. How are we to understand it? 3.27 seems to suggest that though the prophet was dumb for normal purposes, his voice periodically returned, solely to allow him to prophesy. Most interpreters have found it difficult to believe that this dumbness did literally afflict the prophet for this whole period. They have observed that prophecies *are* ascribed to Ezekiel during this period when he is said to have been dumb, and have concluded that any dumbness which he suffered was actually for much briefer periods. 4.27 has sometimes been discounted as an editorial attempt to harmonize the statement about the prophet's dumbness with the attribution to him of prophecies during the period in question. Eichrodt notes that 24.15ff. and 33.21-22 relate to a period of dumbness imposed only shortly before the fall of Jerusalem. He suggests that in the process of editing or transmission this phenomenon has been read back into the beginning of the prophet's ministry.

But it is at least possible that we ought to take the plain meaning of the text more seriously. If the prophet did spend the first few years of his ministry in a more or less permanent state of dumbness this would fit in with the heavy emphasis in Ezekiel on enacted prophecy. It also fits in with the belief that much of Ezekiel's prophecy received written form at a very early stage. Perhaps we really should imagine Ezekiel in these first few years after his call as a generally speechless prophet, who communicated by dramatically acting out his prophecies, or by writing, and perhaps only occasionally burst out with oracular utterances.

Davis connects the story of Ezekiel's dumbness with the account of his eating the scroll at the time of his call. His eating the scroll means that the word of God comes to him already in the form of a written text, and the dumbness expresses the conviction that he is called to *write* his message, not to convey it orally as earlier prophets had done.

3.25 is also rather mysterious: 'and you, O Son of Man, behold, cords will be placed upon you, and you shall be bound with them, so that you cannot go out among the people'. Is this a figurative way of saying that the prophet suffered some kind of paralysis accompanying the dumbness? If a paralysis of some sort is involved, is it connected with the enacted prophecy described in ch. 4, in which Ezekiel claims to have remained prostrate on one side for a very considerable period (over a year, as the text now stands)? In favour of connecting the restraint of 3.25 and the enacted prophecy of 4.4-8 is the fact that both are referred to in the same way. 3.25 says, 'Cords will be placed upon you'. 4.8 says, 'Behold, I will put cords on you'. Another way to interpret these passages is to see them as references to enacted prophecies in which the prophet allowed himself to be physically bound. But this is less plausible than the alternative. Zimmerli suggests that his fellow exiles were the ones who imposed the restraint on Ezekiel, and that this reflects opposition to him. But there is no suggestion elsewhere of such opposition, and if this were the meaning, we might have expected it to be made clear.

The 'binding' mentioned in 3.25 and the dumbness imposed in 3.26 are preceded by a command from God (3.24) to the prophet to shut himself in his house. This may indeed have been a more or less permanent feature of his ministry, since he is never spoken of as prophesying or appearing in any public place. When the location of his activities is specified it is normally at his house. There he is consulted by others (8.1; 14.1; 20.1; 33.30-31). From there he makes his visionary journeys (8.1ff.; 37.1ff.; 40.1ff.). His inaugural vision, however, does apparently take place in the open plain (1.1-3), and in 37.1ff., though it begins at home, the vision of the valley of dry bones is set in the open.

In the period between his call and the second deportation, Ezekiel prophesies that further disaster is yet to come. He does this at least partly through the medium of enacted prophecies. For example, he enacts the conditions of a siege (ch. 4), and in ch. 5 he cuts off all his hair and manipulates it in rather elaborate ways.

We are told in chs. 8–11 of a visionary visit which the

prophet made to Jerusalem during this period before the second deportation. The book offers us a good deal of detail about what the prophet saw there. He witnesses various 'abominations' or cultic irregularities which were going on in the temple area itself. He has a vision of judgment in which the inhabitants of the city are slaughtered, and the experience includes a sight of the divine glory and the throne-chariot, recalling the prophet's inaugural vision. At the end, before the prophet is transported back to Babylonia, the divine glory leaves the city.

As I shall indicate elsewhere, this Jerusalem vision has been much debated, and many interpreters of Ezekiel have concluded that the prophet made a real, terrestrial visit to Jerusalem from Babylon and that he prophesied there.

During the siege of Jerusalem, which led up to its second fall in 586, Ezekiel's wife apparently died (ch. 24). He was instructed by God not to mourn. This seems to be a sign that the loss was to be accepted as God's act.

Once the fall of the city takes place, and the news of it reaches the community in Babylon, Ezekiel is said to be released from his dumbness. At this point in Ezekiel's ministry the tone of his message appears to change. This begins with a phase of what Fohrer calls 'conditional optimism'. It may be that to this period belong some of the oracles against foreign nations. Oracles predicting the punishment of the nations in the prophets not uncommonly accompany those predicting the salvation of Israel and Judah.

But this phase seems to give way to more whole-hearted optimism, in which the prophet envisages the restoration of the people to their land, and the reunion of the two halves of the nation. (See, typically, ch. 36, and the famous vision of the valley of dry bones in ch. 37.)

Of the latter part of Ezekiel's life we have little evidence. If he was aged 30 in 593 at the time of his call he is unlikely to have lived to see the rise of Cyrus and the beginnings of the process of return, and nothing in the book suggests that he did.

The book ends with the lengthy final vision in which the prophet sees the restored temple in the midst of the restored community. In the descriptions of the disposition of this restored community there are enough stylized and idealized features to suggest that the prophet was not facing the practicalities of an imminent restoration. There is no evidence that Ezekiel himself ever returned to the land of his origins.

The Personality of Ezekiel

May we, from what we are told of the prophet's life and times, and from the content of his message, draw any conclusions about his character and personality? Answers to this question vary widely. Rendtorff, in his *Introduction*, sees the book as such a complex literary artefact, with such a long history of overworking, that 'it is virtually impossible to discover much about the person of the prophet' (p. 213). Yet Eissfeldt in his *Introduction*, though acknowledging the existence in the book of non-authentic material, and recognizing extensive editorial overworking, still believes that it gives us genuine information about the real prophet. 'The book gives us a clear and accurate picture of Ezekiel' (p. 381). Perhaps we could say that as long as we exercise due caution, and refrain from dogmatism, a picture emerges from the book which looks credible and is reasonably coherent. That there are tensions within the picture the book gives is not to be disputed, and they are such tensions that many among earlier generations of scholars found the total picture *not* credible.

Ezekiel as he is presented in the book is an ecstatic, who has elaborate and strange visions which are described with extraordinary power. He frequently expresses himself in enactments which vary from the brief but simple (if we include such examples as the hand-clapping and foot-stamping of 6.11) to the extended and bizarre, for instance his enactment of the siege in ch. 4 and his manipulation of his hair in ch. 5.

But Ezekiel also engages in rather lengthy discussions, in precise, legal-sounding terms. He describes in some detail the ground plan of the new temple which is to be rebuilt, and sets out some of the regulations governing the organization and worship of the restored community. He has a strong interest in the priestly language of cleanness and uncleanness. We may not conclude, however, that these are two quite separate and irreconcilable Ezekiels. Even in the descriptions of the visions, the rather pedantic, exact and even laboured detail appears, and many of the oracles and enactments are given precise dates. This suggests that the priestly exactitude and visionary mysticism are features of the same character. Prophetic and priestly elements do not separate out neatly from each other in the book. For example, the prophetic message of forgiveness and salvation is expressed in the cultic language of purification and expiation (see, for instance, 36.24-25). We must also raise the question how far the tensions which we tend to perceive in the book are products of our own expectations. What look to us like incompatible elements may not have appeared so to Ezekiel's contemporaries. And although Ezekiel seems, on any showing, to be a striking and extraordinary figure, in the context of the ancient world and what that world expected of an inspired religious devotee he may have appeared much less remarkable than he seems to a twentieth-century reader.

The Psychology of Ezekiel

It has sometimes been suggested that some of the strange behaviour attributed to Ezekiel in the book is evidence of a psychotic or disordered personality. We have, first, the dumbness, which (if we take the text at its face value) he seems to exhibit for long periods (3.25-26; cf. 33.21-22). There is also the episode in 4.4-8 in which the prophet is alleged to have lain on his left side for 390 days, and then on his right side for 40 days more. This has been interpreted as some kind of paralysis. There are the 'sign-actions', some of which are bizarre or even repulsive. These have already been alluded to (4.9-17; 5.1ff.; cf. 12.17-20; and also 12.3-7). All of these features have been seen as reflecting a psychologically disturbed personality, and some have attempted to be more precise and to put a name to the disorder. It has been asserted that Ezekiel suffered from catalepsy, and from hallucinations, and he has been diagnosed as schizophrenic.

Recent writers on Ezekiel are in general unsympathetic to such suggestions. No reliable diagnosis of the mental state of a character from the past can be arrived at on the basis of the fragmentary records which usually survive. We should need to know far more than we do about Ezekiel before we could draw meaningful conclusions of this sort. K. Jaspers, in an important article in 1947, effectively argued against all attempts to detect pathological states of mind in Ezekiel. Furthermore, though there seem to be, from a twentieth-century point of view, many elements of the bizarre both in Ezekiel's behaviour and in the way he expresses his message, the *content* of that message is entirely rational. If the book at all represents his mind, the prophet was clearly a powerful, profound and courageous thinker, whose influence in reshaping Jewish religion to meet the needs of the postexilic age was extremely strong. It is not plausible that such influence could be exercised by a person of deranged mind.

Further Reading

E. Broome, 'Ezekiel's Abnormal Personality', *JBL* 65 (1946), pp. 277-92.

C.G. Howie, *The Date and Composition of Ezekiel* (SBLMS, 4; Missoula, MT: Scholars Press, 1960), pp. 69-84.

K. Jaspers, 'Der Prophet Ezekiel: Eine pathographische Studie', *Arbeiten zur Psychiatrie, Neurologie und ihren Grenzegebieten. Festschrift K. Schneider* (Heidelberg, 1947), pp. 77-85.

J. Lindblom, *Prophecy in Ancient Israel* (Oxford: Basil Blackwell, 1962), pp. 190-91, 198-99, 206, 261ff.

G. Widengren, *Literary and Psychological Aspects of the Hebrew Prophets* (Uppsala: Uppsala University Press, 1946), ch. 4.

R.R. Wilson, *Prophecy and Society in Ancient Israel* (Philadelphia: Fortress Press, 1980), pp. 282-86.

4

THE HISTORY OF EZEKIEL
CRITICISM: 1900–1950

IT HELPS TO CLARIFY the picture, and to introduce a little
order into the apparent chaos of conflicting critical opinions
about the book of Ezekiel, if we observe that the study of the
book has passed through a number of fairly well defined
phases.

The word 'fairly' must be given due weight. For the sake of
clarity, I shall distinguish three major phases, but for the sake
of accuracy it must be acknowledged that the phases overlap.
Some of the questions characteristic of phase two were being
raised by one or two scholars even while most of their fellows
were still firmly locked in phase one. And there is a greater
overlap, chronologically speaking, between what I am calling
phases two and three, in that a number of scholars have
continued to be preoccupied with phase two approaches some
time after most others had developed their thinking along
phase three lines.

But, while allowing that the phases cannot be too tidily
delineated, it remains of great usefulness to point them out.
During the first phase, whose end coincided almost exactly
with the end of the ninetenth century, the book was seen as
relatively unproblematic. Even after biblical criticism had
become well established and had been applied to many other
Old Testament books, that of Ezekiel was not regarded by the
great majority of scholars as raising any acute or obvious
critical questions. The words of S.R. Driver, in his *Introduction
to the Literature of the Old Testament*, first published in 1891,
have often been quoted, but they are quoted here again since

they sum up so strikingly the perspective of most nineteenth-century scholarship on Ezekiel: 'No critical question arises in connexion with the authorship of the book, the whole from beginning to end bearing unmistakably the stamp of a single mind' (p. 261).

Where English-speaking authors quote Driver, continental scholars usually cite Smend's words, written in 1880, that 'no passage [from Ezekiel] could be removed without endangering the whole structure'. Taken out of context, Smend's words are deceptive, for Smend's strong affirmation of the unity of the book's structure was only possible, for him, at the cost of denying the authenticity of the scheme of dates which the book contains, and regarding many of the prophecies as prophecies after the event.

Even before Smend wrote, Zunz had suggested in 1873 that the book of Ezekiel was a pseudepigraph, written during the Persian period. Seinecke in 1884 developed a theory on similar lines, but dated the work even later, in the time of the Maccabees. Thus was the second phase, that of radical criticism, foreshadowed. Indeed, even further back, in the eighteenth century, Ezekiel criticism had begun (rather mildly, by later standards) with Oeder's questioning (in 1756) of the authenticity of chs. 40–48. He was followed in 1792 by Corrodi, who also rejected chs. 38–39. So Driver's assertion that 'no critical question arises' was not entirely true. Critical questions had arisen.

Nevertheless, the suggestions noted above were rare harbingers, preparing camp for the army of radical ideas shortly to take the field. Driver's confident words really were representative of the bulk of scholarly opinion of his day. Driver's statement contrasts dramatically, however, with the situation which developed within a few years of its publication, when Ezekiel studies were producing theory after theory of the book's origins, each one seemingly more radical than the last. This was the beginning of what I am calling 'phase two'. During the first few decades of this century the diversity of opinions on Ezekiel was astonishing. So diverse were they that almost the only thing about Ezekiel on which scholars appeared to be agreed was that the book did *not* 'bear the stamp of a single mind'. The catalogue of theories emanating from this period is set out below. Comparable accounts may be found in most of the larger works on Old Testament introduction. It is easy, when reading these acounts, to get the impression that Ezekiel criticism is in a state of extraordinary flux, and that there is no unanimity among scholars about the book's origins. It should be appreciated that this is an accurate judgment only on this second phase of Ezekiel studies, and that this phase is now over. If the beginning of the phase can be dated fairly precisely to the turn of the century, its end is less sharply defined. It may, however, be regarded as having worked itself out, more or less, by the end of the 1950s. Though we have by no means reached scholarly unanimity, the disparity between current scholarly views of Ezekiel is much less marked.

This second phase of Ezekiel criticism was dominated by the use of literary-critical techniques. These techniques, which produced such significant results when applied to the Pentateuch and some other narrative literature, were on the whole less strikingly productive when applied to prophecy, and were certainly not notably successful in elucidating the structure and development of the book of Ezekiel. They most assuredly did not produce a scholarly consensus.

In more recent decades, the application of form criticism and the study of tradition history have been more fruitful, and something more like a consensus view appears to be emerging. This is what we may call phase three of Ezekiel criticism.

Radical Criticism of Ezekiel, 1900–circa 1960

The phase of radical criticsm began in earnest in 1900 with the work of Kraetzschmar. Kraetzschmar used the distinction between first-person and third-person materials as a clue to the book's disparate origins. He did not actually challenge the authenticity of either of the strands; he identified them simply as two recensions. Kraetzschmar saw the presence of the several doublets which exist in the book as confirming his view that two parallel forms of the book were to be looked for. The attempt to split Ezekiel into different layers or strands was to be repeated again and again during the next fifty years. A succession of scholars seemed convinced of the necessity of dismembering the work, but they disagreed widely as to the criteria to be employed in doing so. Kraetzschmar was followed swiftly by Budde, who in 1906 advanced a more complex theory of several different recensions, which had eventually been combined. Herrmann (in 1908, and see also his commentary of 1924) still maintained the view that Ezekiel was responsible for most of the material of the book, but abandoned any idea that it had been put together in any ordered way. He saw it as having been built up over a period, from individual passages and shorter collections, perhaps in its earlier stages by the prophet himself, later by others who had expanded it, but all in what was essentially a random fashion.

The first serious challenge to the authenticity of any considerable part of the material of the book was made by Hölscher in 1924. He seems to have taken his cue from Duhm's work on Jeremiah in making his main criterion for analysis the distinction between poetry and prose. The original prophet, Hölscher asserted, was a poet, and therefore it is among the poetic oracles that we should search for his authentic work.

Hölscher did retain some prose as genuinely originating with Ezekiel, namely the account of the prophet's call, and descriptions of prophetic enactments and visions. He rejected some poetry as not being in the metre which Ezekiel generally used. He did also use criteria other than the poetry/prose distinction. He rejected *all* the hopeful material as not original. This excluded the whole of chs. 33–48. He also rejected everything that he thought reminiscent of Deuteronomy (since he ascribed a late date to Deuteronomy) and of the Holiness Code. In sum, the application of Hölscher's criteria involved the rejection of a very large proportion of the book. He was left, indeed, with an authentic core of no more than 170 verses. The additions to this core he saw as having been made principally by an early fifth-century Zadokite redactor, followed by a series of others who supplemented it further. On Hölscher's view, the fifth-century Zadokite is the person really responsible for the book as we have it.

Although Hölscher appears on the surface to be operating with formal, literary criteria (the poetry/prose distinction, Deuteronomistic stylistic features and so on) there is a little below the surface another criterion being applied: this is the distinction between the prophetic and the priestly material. This perceived tension between the prophetic and priestly elements in the book was from Hölscher onwards to be a potent factor in Ezekiel criticism.

The tension was perceived from two angles, some scholars emphasizing the one, some the other. There was first the religious aspect. Many critics saw a sharp and irreconcilable contrast between prophetic and priestly religion, and were unable to believe that the two could really belong together in the same work. But there was also a personal aspect. Many felt that an Ezekiel who could be responsible for the poetic oracles of the first part of the book as well as some of the prosaic, sacerdotal/legal material predominating towards its end was simply not a credible personality.

Torrey's work on Ezekiel, published in 1930, was part of a far-reaching historical reconstruction which challenged the historicity of the whole tradition of the exile. Given that the book of Ezekiel presents the prophet as one whose activities were centred around the exile, Torrey's reconstruction could only be sustained by taking a very radical view of the book.

He suggested that it was a pseudepigraph, the core of the book having been written in the third century BC, about the year 230, but purporting to have been written in the thirtieth year of Manasseh, by a prophet of that period. (The mysterious 'thirtieth year' mentioned in Ezek. 1.1 relates to this.) At a later stage the book was adapted and attributed to the exilic age, and its dates were revised to make it and its ostensible prophetic author fit into its new historical context. On Torrey's view, this prophet had no historical reality. He is an invention of the author of the book. Torrey's views are usually given more attention in the literature on Ezekiel than they deserve. They excite comment because of their outlandish nature, but they were never influential and appear to have attracted few, if any, supporters.

Smith, in 1931, was one who did follow a partly similar line
of argument. Torrey had drawn attention to a number of passages which, he argued, implied a Palestinian background,
not an exilic one, and which betrayed no awareness of any
exile. (These were principally chs. 8–11.) Smith took his cue
from the same passages, but concluded from them, not that
the book was a pseudepigraph purporting to have been
written in the seventh century, but that it genuinely had
been written in the seventh century.
Smith saw Ezekiel, however, as a prophet of *Northern*
Israel. He had been deported in 734 by the Assyrians and
returned to his homeland in 691. He is thus genuinely a
prophet of exile, but it is the earlier exile, that of Northern
Israel, which he represents. Three oracles were delivered to
the Northern exiles (20.32ff., 36.16-32, and 37.11-14); the rest
were addressed to the Northern community in Palestine. Like
Torrey, Smith concluded that the book was later revised to
relate it to the sixth-century exile of the people of Judah.
The work of Torrey and Smith was not altogether a dead
end. Others, too, saw significance in the 'Palestinian' passages
and took them as evidence for a Palestinian ministry. They
did not, however, see them as evidence for a Palestinian ministry at a radically different date from the sixth century in
which the book is ostensibly set.
Herntrich (1932), like some scholars before and after him,
felt it necessary to separate the book into two major strands,
but instead of using linguistic criteria (as, in their different
ways, Kraetzschmar and Hölscher had done), or seeing a distinction between prophetic and priestly elements (Hölscher
again), Herntrich made his criterion the distinction between
the Palestine-based material and the Babylonia-based.
According to Herntrich, the original Ezekiel was a Palestinian
prophet who exercised his ministry in Jerusalem in the years
before 586. The core of chs. 1–39 of the book emanate from
this prophet and period. (Herntrich does leave open the possibility that Ezekiel was with the exiles in Babylon after 586,
but does not believe that any of his surviving prophecies come
from that setting.) The rest of the book is the work of a redactor, a disciple of Ezekiel's living in exile. This redactor not only

added the extra material, but reworked the first 39 chapters
so as to attribute the whole to a prophet based in Babylonia.
But whereas Herntrich wished to turn Ezekiel into a purely
Palestinian prophet, seeing the Babylonian and exilic elements
as due to a redactor, Bertholet (1936) saw the two kinds of
material as representing two ministries, exercised in the two
different milieux by the same prophet. He saw Ezekiel as
having prophesied in Jerusalem from 593 to 586, and in
Babylonia subsequently. The Palestinian deposit was introduced by the scroll vision in 2.3–3.9, while the Babylonian
collection was introduced originally by the vision of the
throne-chariot in 1.4–2.2.

Bertholet took it that Ezekiel himself had compiled the book.
(He believed that the prophet did so in 573, the date
mentioned in 40.1.) It was compiled, he thought, on the basis
of notes made earlier. We do not, however, possess the book in
the form in which it left Ezekiel's hand. Bertholet recognized
that some passages are in inappropriate positions and must
therefore have been placed there secondarily. He also believed
that the text needed substantial correction on the basis of the
Septuagint.

The conclusion that there must have been a Palestinian
ministry was defended by a number of scholars over the next
twenty or thirty years. Spiegel had already anticipated
Herntrich by suggesting it in 1931, and Matthews, at about
the same date as Herntrich, arrived independently at conclusions very similar to Herntrich's own.

Others found themselves more persuaded by Bertholet's
presentation of the matter. Van den Born (1947) saw the first
part of the book as emanating from Palestine, but transferred
the call vision of ch. 1 to the end of ch. 32, seeing ch. 33 as the
beginning of the Babylonian section. Auvray opted for a very
similar line, except that he kept ch. 33 as the closing chapter
of the Palestinian ministry. Robinson, in his *Two Hebrew
Prophets* (1948), also came round to the opinion that Ezekiel
prophesied first in Palestine and then in Babylon.

It is certainly tempting to see Ezekiel's manifest concern for
the Jerusalem community as reflecting an actual ministry

there, and during the 1930s and 1940s the idea that he exercised *some* sort of Palestinian ministry became common enough to be regarded as the prevailing orthodoxy. But the theory took several different forms. It was possible, as Herntrich did, to see Ezekiel as confined to Jerusalem. It was possible to follow Bertholet in postulating a Jerusalem ministry followed by a Babylonian one. And it was possible to see Ezekiel as having received his call in exile, as the book states, but having made one or more visits to his homeland. On this view the accounts of visionary visits to Jerusalem which the book contains reflect actual physical journeys.

All of these were attempts, in different ways, to take seriously the material of apparently Palestinian background which the book contains. During the 1930s and 1940s Cooke (1936) was something of a lone voice in maintaining the theory of an exclusively exilic ministry.

But although the suggestion that Ezekiel exercised a ministry in Palestine, in one form or another, gathered a fair number of supporters, no unanimity had emerged by the end of the 1940s on the more general questions about how the book of Ezekiel should be analysed or how it had come into being. There was widespread agreement that the book was unconvincing as it stood, and numerous attempts had been made to analyse it into different strands; but there were very wide divergences of opinion about how this should be done. Should it be split into different genres of literary material (poetry and prose, for example); or into materials of different dates; or into strata showing different religious perspectives (prophetic and priestly); or into layers with different geographical provenance (Palestinian and Babylonian)? Not only did these different ways of analysing the book produce very different results from each other, but even the application of the same criteria tended to produce different results in different hands.

During the 1940s and 1950s there was a minor revival of theories placing Ezekiel at a date later than the one to which it ostensibly relates. The Norwegian scholar Messel (1945) suggested that the real Ezekiel belonged to the period around 400 BC. He was an exile, but was among those *returning* from

Babylon. Most of the material of chs. 1–24 and 40–48 originated at this date of about 400 BC, but about 50 years later a
redactor not only edited this material but added a great deal
more, contriving in the process to retroject the whole ministry
into the time of the exile.

Van den Born's theory was constructed on similar lines. He
detected evidence that the book was dependent on other texts
known to be postexilic. He therefore dated it to the period of
Ezra and Nehemiah, but thought it had been worked over in
the time of Alexander. He believed that chs. 38–39 referred to
events of that period.

Browne (1952) not only dated the book late, but revived
earlier ideas about its being a pseudepigraph. He believed
that it was actually written during the period of Alexander
the Great, and relates to the arrival of Alexander in the east,
but was deliberately attributed to the exilic prophet Ezekiel.

The failure of scholarship at this stage to produce any sort
of agreement was bound to prompt the thought that there
might be something to be said for the less radical approaches
of the more distant past. There had always, of course, been
scholars who for dogmatic reasons rejected critical methods (I
have not considered these here). But from the 1950s onwards
there is detectable in Ezekiel criticism, at least in some
quarters, the feeling that if none of the radical theories had
commanded a consensus, then perhaps there was something
to be said for less adventurous views.

Howie, in 1950, rejected all the arguments for a Palestinian
ministry and confined the prophet's work to Babylon and to
the years 593–567. Mullo-Weir independently arrived at
similar conclusions. The approach of Pfeiffer in his
Introduction to the Old Testament also seems to reflect the
new mood. Pfeiffer rejects all the more radical theories and
takes the book to be 'substantially trustworthy' (p. 535). He
thinks it likely that the prophet prepared at least one edition of
his own book. Part of it consists of public addresses, and about
half (parts of chs. 1–24 and 33–39, and the whole of chs. 25–
32 and 40–48) of written compositions, never delivered orally.

Pfeiffer does accept the idea of a Palestinian ministry. Not
only did Ezekiel prophesy in Jerusalem before 587 (during

which period he wrote very little, but addressed people by word of mouth) but he returned to Jerusalem for a time, even after his call in Babylon. During his Babylonian ministry he not only addressed his fellow exiles mostly in writing but put into written form his earlier speeches. Pfeiffer identifies three distinct stages in the building up of the book. He actually speaks of its having been compiled in three 'volumes'. But he regards Ezekiel himself as having been responsible for all three volumes. He leaves open the question of whether Ezekiel also combined the three volumes into a single work or whether this was done by a later hand. Pfeiffer allows for relatively modest additions to the book after Ezekiel's own time, his suspicions focusing mainly on chs. 38–39. The dislocations and doublets which the book manifestly contains are due to redactors of the late sixth and early fifth centuries.

It is clear that with Pfeiffer Ezekiel criticism is shifting into much more sober mood. True, he does not accept the book simply at face value. He takes it that the prophet really did operate in Jerusalem, though the book implies he did not. He allows for a process of compilation in several stages. He allows for editorial work and additions later than Ezekiel's time. But the bulk of the material is seen as genuinely representing the mind of Ezekiel, and Ezekiel is accepted as an exilic prophet, belonging to the very period in which the book assumes him to have been placed.

It must not be supposed that the mood signalled by Pfeiffer was shared by all scholars, or that the 1950s marked the definitive end of phase two of Ezekiel studies. Herrmann (1965) is still unconvinced of the substantial unity of the book, but proposes a fresh criterion. The original Ezekiel was a prophet of doom: oracles of salvation and promise are attributed to a later hand.

But from the 1950s onwards, although some of the same problems were still felt, form-critical and traditio-historical critical methods became much more prominent in attempts to find answers to them. With the application of these methods we are moving into what I have labelled phase three of Ezekiel studies. Pfeiffer's work is transitional. In his conclusions he anticipates phase three developments, but his methods are still very much those of the previous phase. Pfeiffer is a literary critic through and through, and his thinking is as yet untouched by form-critical and traditio-historical developments.

But before proceeding to describe phase three, certain observations are worth making about what I have called phase two. One reason why some of the heat has gone out of Ezekiel studies is that present-day scholars see the difficulties of the book of Ezekiel as much less overwhelming than did many of their predecessors. To understand the burst of radical theories about the book which prevailed during the first half of this century we need to ask why it was that scholars of that period found the book so problematic.

Part of the answer is to be found in the views which were then current about the nature of Israelite religion. The idea of 'progressive revelation' dominated the thinking of many biblical scholars, and the religion of the Old Testament tended to be seen as a progression towards an ever more refined understanding of God. Ezekiel in several respects fits badly into such a scheme. What was taken to be his emphasis on individual responsiblity was certainly seen as fitting into the line of forward development, but other features of his work seemed to be regressive rather than progressive. His legalism and his interest in the cult were not at that period evaluated very positively. His serious concern with such subjects as ritual uncleanness, and his failure to distinguish sharply between moral offences and ritual or cultic ones, were seen as examples of the kind of religious attitudes from which enlightened prophets had moved away. 'Ethical monotheism' is not an entirely convincing label for what is preached in the book of Ezekiel. Biblical scholars and students during the early decades of this century were inclined to see a very clear constrast between prophetic religion (good) and priestly religion (on the whole rather bad). Taking such a view they were bound to be embarrassed by Ezekiel, who as the book presents him to us is manifestly both prophet *and* priest, and shared the characteristics of both. Furthermore, even as a prophet Ezekiel was bound to look a little suspect, for in most of the so-called 'writing prophets' features such as ecstasy, and the use of prophetic enactments, do not appear to be prominent. These were perceived by scholars of the generation in question as among the more primitive features of prophecy, which were being left behind. But in Ezekiel such features abound, and the prophet is presented as one who displayed ecstasy in some quite extreme forms, and indulged in behaviour that was often quite bizarre.

In addition to all this, to take the book at its face value would mean crediting Ezekiel with powers such as clairvoyance and/or telepathy and possibly even levitation. It appears that the prophecies were uttered or written in exile, yet he describes in some detail events which he says are taking place in Jerusalem, and speaks on one occasion of being lifted up by his hair and taken to Jerusalem on a visit (8.3). In the rationalistic intellectual climate of the early twentieth century such claims were bound to be regarded unsympathetically. The problems they raised were, as we have seen, dealt with by various theories about when and where the prophet exercised his ministry. The problems of the tension between the prophetic and the priestly characteristics of Ezekiel, as well as those presented by the diversity of the material in the book, were addressed by the various attempts to dismember the book, and/or Ezekiel himself, which have been catalogued above. Ezekiel, as the book presents him, was simply not seen, by many scholars, as a credible personality: hence the dismemberment.

A conclusion which may be drawn from all this is that the problems which were, in the first half of this century, perceived in Ezekiel arose to a considerable extent not directly from the book itself, but from the presuppositions with which it was approached.

Further Reading

S.R. Driver, *An Introduction to the Literature of the Old Testament* (Edinburgh: T. & T. Clark, 2nd edn, 1891).

G. Hölscher, *Hesekiel, der Dichter und das Buch* (BZAW, 38; Giessen: Töpelmann, 1924).

W.A. Irwin, *The Problem of Ezekiel* (Chicago: Chicago University Press, 1943).

—'Ezekiel Research since 1943', *VT* 3 (1953), pp. 54-66.

C.J. Mullo-Weir, 'Aspects of the Book of Ezekiel', *VT* 2 (1952), pp. 97-112.

R.H. Pfeiffer, *Introduction to the Old Testament* (London: A. & C. Black, 1953), pp. 518-73.

H.W. Robinson, *Two Hebrew Prophets* (London: Lutterworth, 1948).

H.H. Rowley, 'The Book of Ezekiel in Modern Study', *BJRL* 36 (1953–54), pp. 146-90. Reprinted in *Men of God* (London: Nelson, 1963), pp. 169-210.

C.C. Torrey, *Pseudo-Ezekiel and the Original Prophecy* (New Haven: Yale University Press, 1930; repr. New York: Ktav, 1970).

See also the general introductions to the Old Testament listed at the end of the next chapter.

5

THE HISTORY OF EZEKIEL CRITICISM: THE 1950s TO THE PRESENT DAY

IF PHASE TWO of Ezekiel criticism petered out rather untidily in mid-century, we may identify the year 1955 as a fairly decisive beginning for phase three. 1955 saw the publication of the first fascicle of Zimmerli's monumental commentary and also a major commentary by Georg Fohrer, though Fohrer's position had already been outlined in 1952 in an important monograph, *Die Hauptprobleme des Buches Ezekiel*. In the years following, contributions were made to the debate about Ezekiel by a number of major scholars, and although these were certainly not unanimous in their conclusions, the extent of the common ground which they shared was, after the chaos of phase two, striking. These scholars represented, at last, a degree of consensus, though as we shall see, the consensus was by no means universal.

The main features of this new consensus are as follows:

1. There is a considerable degree of acceptance of the book's ostensible placing of the original prophet in the context of the exile, and an impatience with attempts to date him elsewhere.
2. There is a general abandonment of theories that locate Ezekiel's ministry, in part or in whole, anywhere other than Babylonia. The consensus position on these first two points is well summed up by Eissfeldt in his *Introduction*: 'So far as the period and the place of the prophet's activity are concerned, we must be satisfied with the remark that there are no really decisive arguments against the reliability of the tradition which finds

expression in many passages in the book, particularly
with regard to the dating. These show Ezekiel as having
been called to be a prophet in the exile in 593 and as
having been active there as such until 573 or perhaps
somewhat longer. All the hypotheses which have been
proposed in place of this labour under much greater
difficulties than does the traditional view' (p. 372).

3. There is a general disillusionment with, and abandonment of, the purely literary-critical techniques which
   characterized phase two, and an espousal of form-
   critical and tradition-history methods.
4. There is a readiness to accept that there is a substantial
   body of material which goes back to the prophet himself
   or at least to the exilic period close to his lifetime.
5. There is a disinclination to split up the priestly and the
   prophetic elements in the book.
6. There is a very widespread recognition that however
   the core of material original to the prophet and to the
   exilic period is defined, it has received considerable
   additions and expansions, probably in a multiplicity of
   stages and over a very long period.

I shall now examine the work of one or two scholars whose
views are typical of this broad consensus, and outline their
conclusions. The first is Georg Fohrer. What Fohrer sees as
the principal problem of the book of Ezekiel is stated in his
Introduction as follows:

> He [Ezekiel] always appears primarily as a prophet to Judah
> and Jerusalem, although he lives among the deportees in
> Babylonia. Since it is almost impossible to imagine such a
> prophet, it was natural that this view should arouse doubts.

Although he sees this problem as a large and insistent one,
Fohrer does not see any value in radical theories that alter
the place or period of Ezekiel's ministry. He concludes firmly
that there is no evidence for dating the book at any other
period than the one to which it purports to belong. He likewise dismisses attempts to confine Ezekiel's ministry to
Palestine, finding it implausible that if Ezekiel *had* been a
Palestinian prophet, the book could have been so thoroughly

revised as to produce the appearance of a ministry in Babylon. Nor is Fohrer impressed with the various attempts to reconstruct a double ministry for Ezekiel, part in Jerusalem, part in Babylon.

Fohrer himself accepts that Ezekiel was deported in 597, and called to prophesy in 593 or 592. He accepts the originality of the dating series, according to the regnal years of Jehoiachin (who was still seen as legitimate ruler). He sees Ezekiel's ministry as confined to Babylonia, as the book suggests. But the prophet's message, in spite of appearances, was directed towards the exiles among whom he was living.

Traditio-historical study suggests that later editors and redactors have imposed their own interpretations on the material, reflecting the interests of their own times. Once these later interpretations are recognized, some of the problems with which earlier generations of scholars wrestled are removed. Thus the problem that Ezekiel, a prophet in exile, devotes so much of his attention to the Palestinian and Jerusalem community is removed by Fohrer when he concludes that Ezekiel's oracles are *not* addressed to the Palestinian/Jerusalem community after all. They have only been made to look as if they are. Some other difficulties disappear in the same way, notably when the results are recognized of a 'Zadokite' overworking.

Fohrer takes a fairly conservative view of the proportion of material in the book that is genuinely by the prophet Ezekiel, though he does acknowledge some later additions, as we have seen. He does see evidence that some of the material was delivered orally, but he thinks that Ezekiel wrote down his own sayings, and later added expansions of his own.

The dates which appear in the book apply to the sections immediately following them, but other material, not relating to those specific dates, has been spliced in. Some of this splicing, according to Fohrer, was done by Ezekiel himself. Fohrer therefore attributes a good deal less to editorial revision than some other critics. He distinguishes a number of primary collections, which have been put together at an editorial stage. These primary collections, as here delineated, contain within them a number of additions. The primary collections which he identifies may be briefly listed here:

1.1–3.15	The prophet's call
chs. 4–5	Reports of symbolic actions
ch. 6	Sayings collected around a catchword (the catchword being 'idol')
ch. 7	Judgment sayings
8.1–11.13	Accounts of visionary and ecstatic experiences (with an appendix in 11.14-21)
12.1-20	Symbolic actions
12.21–13.21	Sayings about the reliability of prophetic utterances
ch. 14	Two isolated utterances
chs. 15–20	Sayings concerning sin, judgment and responsibility
ch. 21	Sayings with the catchword 'sword'
ch. 22	Blood guilt and individual sin
ch. 23	Oholah and Oholibah
ch. 24	Symbolic actions
ch. 25	A collection of sayings concerning countries in the neighbourhood of Judah
chs. 26–28	Sayings concerning Tyre
chs. 29–32	Sayings concerning Egypt
ch. 33	Sayings from the second period of Ezekiel's ministry
ch. 34	Sayings concerning shepherds and sheep
ch. 35	Sayings concerning Edom
chs. 36–39	The new Israel
chs. 40–48	The rebuilding of Israel

It may be doubted whether the principal problem to which Fohrer addresses himself is quite such an overwhelming one as he makes it out to be. He insists that 'it is almost impossible to imagine' a prophet living in exile, but still primarily concerned with his compatriots in the homeland. But why should this be so difficult to imagine? Why should not a prophet and priest in exile have his interests firmly fixed in his homeland, since it *was* his home, and since it was the place where, throughout the first half of his ministry, the temple which was so important to him still stood?

Greenberg, in the introduction to his commentary, says, 'That Ezekiel in exile should be preoccupied with Jerusalem's fate is not astonishing'. Even the fact that he appears to be *addressing* a Jerusalem audience is not difficult to explain. Much of the time Ezekiel speaks simply to 'the house of

Israel', which appears to cover Palestinian and exiled communities indiscriminately. But even when he explicitly speaks to the inhabitants of Jerusalem this is not, for Greenberg, a problem. He cites as a parallel the example of prophetic oracles against foreign nations. These are formally addressed to the foreign nations themselves, but the real audience is the prophet's compatriots.

We might also cite the example (which Greenberg does not) of Deutero-Isaiah's polemic against idolatry. The mockery is directed towards the idolaters, but it is doubtful whether the idolaters heard it, or would have been touched by it if they had. The people the prophet is really trying to convince are again his own people. His argument is framed to appeal to those who, at bottom, shared his own cultural presuppositions.

What these examples show is that the ostensible audience is not necessarily the real audience. The words which Ezekiel, on the face of it, is addressing to the Jerusalem community might still be intended to be heard primarily by people closer at hand.

The way in which Ezekiel's interest, and the interest of the book, focus so consistently on the Jerusalem community and its fate is nevertheless one of the most remarkable features of the work. It is remarkable because Jeremiah had already, in his prophecy of the good figs, suggested that the exilic community was the true Israel and that the future lay with them (unless, indeed, this prophecy is a later addition to Jeremiah's book). It is remarkable because that view of the matter seems quickly to have come to dominate the thinking of postexilic Judaism. If the picture given in the book of a prophet located in Babylon but having an abiding interest in Jerusalem and directing his prophecies towards Judah were not a true one, there would have been little incentive in the climate of opinion at the time to invent it. Fohrer says in his *Introduction* that, 'the traditional view of the prophet of the exile, with his mind fixed on Judah and Jerusalem, has certainly proved untenable' (p. 405). I do not find this view untenable at all.

The views of Artur Weiser, as outlined in the fourth edition of his *Introduction* (1957), have many points of contact with those of Fohrer. Like Fohrer, Weiser sees the dated series of oracles as original, though he acknowledges that unrelated material has been secondarily inserted into the series. He is prepared to entertain the suggestion, originating with Eissfeldt, that there were in fact *two* dated series, one of oracles on Judah and Jerusalem and one of oracles on foreign nations, the two series having been telescoped editorially.

For the development of the book as a whole Weiser postulates a three-stage process: (1) two different kinds of material were written by the prophet: (a) dated oracles against Judah and Jerusalem and also against foreign nations, and (b) additional undated material; (2) a redactor placed *all* material into a chronological framework and put the oracles against foreign nations in their present position; (3) later expansions and additions were made. Weiser explicitly accepts both the prophetic and the priestly elements in Ezekiel as original.

Weiser's reconstruction of the way in which the book of Ezekiel took shape is broadly representative of what I have called phase three of Ezekiel criticism. There was still plenty of disagreement about the details, but Weiser's reconstruction is fairly typical of the lines along which many scholars were thinking.

Weiser's views on Ezekiel may profitably be compared with those of Otto Eissfeldt, as outlined in the second German edition of his *Introduction* (1955). They are by no means identical with Weiser's but there is a recognizable 'family likeness'. Eissfeldt stresses that the development of the book was a long-drawn-out process. Nevertheless, 'the book clearly contains a framework of passages deriving from the prophet himself'. The criterion which Eissfeldt uses for distinguishing this original framework is the use of the first-person form. Eissfeldt believes that he can detect a coherent series of original oracles, individually dated, and mostly in correct order. These oracles, together with the call vision of 1.1–3.15, the vision in chs. 8–11 in which the prophet visits Jerusalem, the episode in ch. 20 (which Eissfeldt interprets as the rejection of a plan to build a cultic centre in exile) and the vision of Yahweh's re-entry to Jerusalem in chs. 40–48 'all present in a sense a continuous development'. The sequence of the dated sections, and in particular the four which refer to the fate of the temple, 'can only be ascribed to Ezekiel'.

Undated material from other sources has been inserted into this structure, usually at points appropriate to the subject matter. Eissfeldt differs from some other scholars in asserting that this insertion is unlikely to have been done by the prophet himself. Some of the material so inserted may well be genuine. Some of it duplicates, or partly duplicates, material in the dated sections and is therefore presumably original material passed down by a different route. Some of it is not derived from the prophet at all.

The views outlined above are those of three important scholars whose conclusions were typical of this phase of Ezekiel criticism. In reaching such conclusions the methods and techniques of form criticism and of tradition history played a very significant part. It is the contribution of these techniques and methods which we must now examine in a little more detail.

The application of form criticism and tradition history to the book of Ezekiel can best be illustrated by summarizing the work of Zimmerli, who has been its principal exponent. Zimmerli has made a very thoroughgoing form-critical and traditio-historical analysis of the book, tracing its dependence on existing forms and traditions. He has also explored what might be called the socio-legal setting of the material. He has, in addition, done perhaps more than any other scholar to develop the theory of the text's 'after-life', and to trace the process of accretion by which it was expanded. This expansion often involves reinterpretation, and takes a variety of forms. Zimmerli identifies three stages in the composition of the book of Ezekiel: (1) oral delivery by the prophet. Zimmerli finds the oral form still detectable; (2) writing down by the prophet himself; (3) a multiplicity of stages of redaction and addition, the earlier phases of which may be due to the prophet himself, the later ones to a school of traditors. The distinction between the two is by no means always clear.

The existence of an 'Ezekiel school' is fundamental to Zimmerli's understanding of the process of composition of the

book. Zimmerli sees the process of composition as one of
'constant interpretative rewriting' (the phrase is Rendtorff's).
The existence of an Ezekiel school explains why, though the
process continued over a long period, the book has managed to
retain its character and relative coherence.

Much of what is most characteristic of Zimmerli's work on
Ezekiel can be found in accessible form in his 1965 article,
'The Special Form- and Traditio-Historical Character of
Ezekiel'. Near the beginning of this article, Zimmerli makes a
significant statement:

> We will proceed in this task [of elucidating the form and mat-
> erial of the book] from the opinion that even though a complex
> redactional work can be recognized in the book of Ezekiel, it
> preserves for us on the whole the peculiar characteristics of the
> prophet.

Significant here is the preposition 'from': 'We will proceed...
from the opinion that...' Zimmerli's conviction that the book
genuinely gives us access to the mind of Ezekiel is not a
conclusion drawn from form-critical and traditio-historical
study, but a conviction from which the form-critical and
traditio-historical study begins. As Zimmerli sees it, however,
what emerges from form-critical and traditio-historical study
is consistent with his initial presupposition.

Zimmerli, and he is by no means alone in this, attaches
great significance to the speeches in first-person form. The
series of first-person speeches provides the basic structure of
the book. The fact that they are in the first person is a clue
which encourages us to think that they were formulated by
the prophet himself. Zimmerli finds 52 such units. Of the 52
units five are visions; one (the account of the arrival of the
news of Jerusalem's fall, 33.21-22) is peculiar, in that it is
pure narrative with no word of proclamation. Of the
remaining 46, all but one (the lament in ch. 19) are introduced
by the same formula, 'and the word of the Lord came to me'.
This is strictly a narrative formula. It is common in narratives in Samuel and Kings, describing early prophecy, but it
then disappears until it reappears with Jeremiah (1.2; 14.1;
27.12 amongst others) and Ezekiel.

Zimmerli compares with this another phrase, 'the hand of

the Lord was upon me'. This also is a phrase characteristic of pre-classical prophetic literature; after that it appears once in Isaiah (8.11) and once in Jeremiah (15.17), but is employed frequently in Ezekiel.

Zimmerli also notes other features which connect Ezekiel with the pre-classical prophets, namely the coming of the spirit (*rûah*) on the prophet, and the references to translocation.

The use of the phrases 'and the word of the Lord came to me' and 'the hand of the Lord was upon me' point to a feature that is highly characteristic of the book of Ezekiel. The coming of the prophetic word is seen as a *happening*, as a word-*event*. This characteristic also shows itself in the great emphasis which we find in the book on what Zimmerli calls 'sign-actions'. These 'sign-actions' are what used to be called in an earlier generation 'prophetic symbolism', and which it has become more fashionable to refer to as 'prophetic enactments'. Again we find a connection with pre-classical prophecy. Prophetic enactments are frequent in the narratives about the pre-classical prophets. They are, however, relatively infrequent later. We have three examples in Isaiah and seven in Jeremiah, but 12 in Ezekiel. The Ezekiel examples are 3.22-27; 4.1-3; 4.4-8; 4.9-11; 4.12-15; 5.1-3; 12.1-16; 12.17-20; 21.11-12; 21.23-29; 24.15-24 and 37.15-28.

The concentration on the word-event can also be exemplified in the use of the formula 'set your face against...' Several times the prophet is commanded to 'set his face against' the person against whom his prophecies are directed. This is not, says Zimmerli, purely metaphorical. He envisages the prophet actually turning towards the object of his prophesying and delivering his words against it. The phrase does not occur in classical prophecy other than Ezekiel, but it does recall the stories of Balaam in the book of Numbers. See especially Num. 22.41; 23.13 and 24.1-2.

Zimmerli also finds a significant link between Ezekiel and pre-classical prophetic narrative in parallels between certain passages in Ezekiel (8.1ff.; 14.1ff.; 20.1ff [cf. 33.31]) on the one hand and 2 Kgs 6.32. In each case the prophet is sitting 'in his house' and elders are 'sitting with him' or 'sitting before him'. Zimmerli calls this the prophetic *Lehrhaus*. It suggests that the prophet held a kind of 'surgery' at which he was available for formal consultation.

Another type of saying that Zimmerli identifies, which may also give us information about the way in which the prophet operated, is the 'disputation' form, which is common in Ezekiel but does not appear elsewhere in prophetic literature until it is developed by Malachi. One of the important features of the disputation form, according to Zimmerli, is that it cites what other people are saying, so that we find out something of the situation which the prophet was trying to meet. A famous example is ch. 18, where a proverb is quoted in which the people were expressing their disillusionment: 'The parents have eaten sour grapes, and the children's teeth are set on edge'. The rest of the chapter is a discussion in which the prophet takes issue with them. He takes up further complaints later in the same chapter, which are quoted at 18.25 and 18.29. Other examples of disputations are 12.21-28; 33.10ff. and 37.11-14.

There is also a form in which the prophet is asked by the Lord to 'judge' the people (16.4; 20.4; 22.2; 23.36) or to 'make known to them their abominations' (16.2; 20.4; 22.2). This gives us no clear indication, however, of the precise manner in which the judgment was to be made known.

Zimmerli also thinks that the prophet is called upon to accuse people of specific transgressions of law, of which he sees antecedents in Hos. 4.1 and Jer. 7.9. The law against which Ezekiel sees his people as transgressing seems to be related, in Zimmerli's view, to the Holiness code.

Zimmerli makes the further point in his article that Ezekiel very frequently uses the work of earlier prophets as a jumping-off point, either for his 'sermons' or for his sign-actions. For example Jer. 15.16 speaks of 'eating' the word of the Lord and finding it sweet (cf. Ps. 19.11; 119.103). In Ezekiel's call this figure of speech 'becomes a dramatic reality'. Similarly, Ezekiel's enacted prophecy with the hair in ch. 5 seems to take its cue from Isa. 7.20. In both these cases it appears that what is for the earlier prophet a divine word becomes for Ezekiel a word-event.

Zimmerli asks, and answers his own question in the

affirmative, whether the judgment passage in Ezekiel 7, with its keyword in 7.2, 'the end has come', is a development of Amos 8.2. He also sees Ezekiel's parables in chs. 16 and 23 as developing the theme of the unfaithful wife, taken directly from Hosea.

Some of the material of the book of Ezekiel, however, displays the forms not of earlier prophecy but of a quite different kind of tradition; that of sacral law. In a number of passages Zimmerli sees evidence of the 'priestly casuistic style'. What Ezekiel seems to have done is to take over many traditional forms, features and themes from earlier (often very much earlier) prophecy, but to develop this prophetic tradition by drawing on priestly forms, themes and modes of expression.

Ezek. 14.1-11 is a passage whose style, says Zimmerli, 'has grown formally out of sacral law'. Similar features appear in the passages which develop the watchman theme (3.19; 33.9; cf. 33.2; 33.6; 14.13). Chapter 18, the discussion of the righteous man who has an unrighteous son and a righteous grandson, also exhibits characteristics drawn from sacral law.

Both chs. 14 and 18, claims Zimmerli, rest on models derived from priestly discussions of case law. Each hypothetical case is followed first by a verdict, and then by a sentence, or declaration of the person's fate. So we have the alternatives, 'He is righteous' (verdict), 'He shall surely live' (declaration of his fate); or 'He has done all these abominable things' (verdict), 'He shall surely die' (sentence). Zimmerli and von Rad have both suggested that the formula 'He is righteous; he shall surely live' is adapted from an 'entrance liturgy'. Cf. Ps. 118.19-20, and also Pss. 15.1-2 and 24.3-4.

Other features of priestly language identified in Ezekiel 18 are lists of sins and virtues, for example in 18.5-9 and 18.10-13 (cf. 22.6-12; 25.29 and 33.15). These can be paralleled in Lev. 19.11ff., Pss. 15.2-5 and 24.4.

Finally, I must mention a type of saying which is highly characteristic of Ezekiel on which Zimmerli has laid considerable emphasis. These are expressions which are attributed to Yahweh, speaking in the first person, and which have been called 'recognition formulae', 'self-revelation formulae', or 'utterances of God's self-demonstration'. They include the phrases 'I, the Lord, have spoken', 'I am the Lord', and, more characteristically, the expanded form of the latter formula, 'that they (or 'he' or 'you') may know that I am the Lord'. Such phrases point to the way in which God's words or actions function as demonstrations or authentications of his authority and his deity. Zimmerli sees these formulae, like several other features of Ezekiel, as having roots in pre-classical prophecy. He places great weight on 1 Kgs 20.13 and 28 where a similar formula occurs. The validity of this parallel with 1 Kings 20 has, however, been questioned, notably by Fohrer, who thinks it likely that the presence of the formula in 1 Kings 20 is due to a Deuteronomic editor and is not rooted in ancient prophetic tradition at all. However this may be, these 'utterances of God's self-demonstration' certainly appear very frequently in the book of Ezekiel, and embody a key feature of the theology of the Ezekiel tradition.

What do all these observations add up to?

1. They point to connections with pre-classical prophecy, which in any case can be substantiated on other grounds. But they also point to connections with priestly tradition.
2. They enable us to identify important elements which give structure and coherence to the book.
3. They give us some indication of the *Sitz im Leben* in which the prophet's words were uttered. These indications are consistent with the sixth-century exilic setting in which the book is ostensibly placed.
4. They highlight some important elements in Ezekiel's theology.
5. In particular, they heighten our awareness of the intense concentration of the Ezekiel tradition on the 'word-event'. This motif is a unifying factor in the thinking to which the book gives expression.
6. In Zimmerli's mind all these observations are consistent with the existence of a 'school' which developed the Ezekiel tradition over a considerable period.

R.E. Clements, in his essay 'The Ezekiel Tradition: Prophecy in a Time of Crisis', has argued convincingly that just as the

book of Jeremiah has been put into its present form by
someone who was addressing the situation in Judah in the
immediate post-586 situation, so the book of Ezekiel has been
shaped by a person or persons addressing the situation in the
gôlâh (the community in exile) in the period shortly before
538 (or at the latest 516). These shapers of the tradition were,
like Ezekiel himself, rooted in the priestly traditions of
Jerusalem. Clements sums up, 'If our thesis is supportable,
then it would suggest that our prophetic literature has not
been the subject of a more or less continuous and indiscrimi-
nate process of elaboration, commenting and glossing. Rather
a very much more restricted activity has been undertaken,
which can for the most part be assigned a relatively precise
chronological location' (p. 133).

Clements is unhappy with the idea of prophetic 'schools',
either in connection with Ezekiel or with any other prophet. If
his interpretation of the evidence is correct, then Zimmerli's
idea of a process of *Nachinterpretation*, extending over a long
period and through a multiplicity of stages, would require
modification.

It is sometimes said that the scholars of what I have called
'phase three' of Ezekiel studies returned to a more conservative view of the book. The word 'conservative' is in a sense
appropriate, but at the same time misleading. It is appropriate in that scholars of this group returned to taking seriously
the book's own ostensible historical setting, and saw the
traditions it contains as relating to a prophet of the sixth
century, who exercised his whole prophetic ministry in exile,
and who is likely to have been responsible, initially, for a
significant portion of the book's material.

But all the 'phase three' scholars see the book as having
been added to, developed and re-edited, and understand it as
a multi-layered structure. In their willingness to recognize a
diversity of origins and the influence of a multiplicity of hands
in its composition they have much in common with the more
radical-looking scholars of phase two, and are in this respect
anything but 'conservative'.

What mainly marks off the exponents of the phase three
consensus from their immediate predecessors is that those

who in the first half of the century analysed the book into strata of various sorts saw the relationship between any genuine sixth-century core and its accretions as one of *discontinuity*. They saw the book as having been built up largely by the addition of matter which was essentially alien to the core material. The scholars of the consensus which began to emerge in the 1950s and 1960s tend to see the growth of the Ezekiel tradition as essentially one of *continuity*. They envisage the tradition as, in a sense, growing from within, rather than being added to from without. It is not the case, therefore, that the scholars of phase three really visualize the processes of the book's compilation in such a sharply different way from their predecessors. It is rather that they evaluate them differently.

Since the 'consensus' of what I have called phase three of Ezekiel criticism was arrived at, a number of further developments have taken place, leading to considerable diversification in Ezekiel studies. This diversification may at first sight seem to resemble the variety of competing views which marked the first half of the twentieth century, but the diversity is not so much a diversity of conclusions, reached by scholars all using ostensibly similar methods. It is rather a diversity of approaches. Scholars are not, for the most part, giving different answers to the same questions. They are approaching the book from quite different directions.

There is one group of scholars who do appear at first sight to be taking us back to something reminiscent of phase two. The pace-setters of this group are H. Schultz and J. Garscha, although the names of H. Simian, F.L. Hossfeld and G. Bettenzoli should be mentioned in the same connection.

Schultz, writing in 1969, separated out from the book of Ezekiel a series of passages which he believed to relate directly to the historical situation of the sixth century. These must form the basis for reconstructing Ezekiel's original message. These passages consist basically of chs. 4–7, 9, 12, 13, 15–16, 19, 21 and 23–24.

Schultz then identifies a second series of passages which have in common a recognition of the sacral law tradition. These are 3.17-21; 14.1-11, 12-20; 18.1-20; 21.1-16; 33.1-20.

He observes that the first series, anchored in the sixth-century historical situation, reflects no knowledge of the sacral law. The second series, rooted in the sacral law, has no clear points of contact with the sixth-century historical situation. The second series of passages Schultz calls 'the deutero-Ezekielic basic stratum', and sees it as the main secondary layer of material added to the sixth-century core. Garscha (1974) builds on Schultz's work, but has produced a more far-reaching reconstruction which recognizes only a very small sixth-century core. Only 17.1-10 and 23.2-25, he thinks, derive from Ezekiel himself. This small core was expanded greatly in the early fifth century. As compared with Schultz, therefore, Garscha is introducing an extra major stage of expansion. It is this fifth-century stage which introduced the dual ministry, with a preaching of judgment prior to the fall of Jerusalem in 586 and preaching of salvation afterwards. It also introduced the dating system. The material which Schultz ascribes to the sacral law tradition Garscha also recognizes, but claims that it was not incorporated into the book until about 300 BCE.

Schultz and Garscha may appear to be reverting to older approaches to the book of Ezekiel, and indeed they do show a willingness to dismember the book in ways that are reminiscent of older scholarship, but their techniques are significantly different. They employ chiefly the form-critical and traditio-historical methods of such scholars as Fohrer, Weiser and Zimmerli, but arrive at conclusions which challenge the consensus of those other scholars.

It is fundamental to the work of Schultz and Garscha that a sharp distinction is to be made between the prophetic and priestly strands of Ezekiel, whereas majority opinion from about 1950 onwards seemed to be happy to hold them together. The ghost of the Zadokite redactor, who entered the scene at least as early as the time of Hölscher, has not yet been laid.

Rendtorff has gone on record as deploring the way in which both Schultz and Garscha have made use of the term 'Deutero-Ezekiel', firstly because they do not use the phrase in the same way as each other, and secondly because in neither case does it correspond well with the way in which we use the terms 'Deutero-Isaiah' and 'Deutero-Zechariah'. These last terms denote major sections of the canonical books, not redactional levels.

The work of Schultz, Garscha, Hossfeld and similar scholars, though it seems to be addressing old questions, may be regarded in one sense as arising out of the earlier consensus. There was a consensus that the original sixth-century core of the book has been subjected to expansion over a considerable period and through a multitude of stages, but there never was substantial agreement about the details of this process. It is in attempting to reach a more precise understanding of the stages of expansion that Schultz and Garscha have developed their ideas.

Other workers in the field have looked for entirely different starting points. There are those who prefer to leave aside the whole analytical enterprise and treat the book 'holistically'. 'Holistic interpretation' is a phrase used by M. Greenberg, whose major commentary in the Anchor Bible Series (1983) exemplifies it. Greenberg does not exactly dismiss traditional critical analysis, but he is very impatient with what he sees as its shortcomings, and professes to be doing something different. One can appreciate why he might wish to do this. Zimmerli's massive commentary might be said to have done the analytical, form-critical and traditio-historical job definitively for this generation. Any commentator who attempted the same task in the same way at this time would be in danger of producing a largely redundant work. Greenberg has opted for a different approach, and has certainly shown that to take the text as it stands and to attempt to interpret the book as it is, in its final form, can be productive of many insights.

The attempt to consider the text 'as it stands' cannot really leave critical issues on one side, as it is sometimes claimed to do, for the way the text is handled often presupposes or implies particular answers to critical questions. Greenberg, for example, looks for structures and patterns in the book of Ezekiel which, if they are correctly identified, must imply that the book has been shaped by a single mind. Greenberg appears to assume that the single mind is that of the prophet, but this needs more discussion than Greenberg gives it. He says tentatively at the end of his introduction to volume 1 of the commentary that,

> The persuasion grows on one, as piece after piece falls into the established patterns and ideas, that a coherent world of vision is emerging, contemporary with the sixth-century prophet and decisively shaped by him, if not the very words of Ezekiel himself.

This seems to leave open the possibility that other hands and minds may have been engaged in the formation of the book as we have it, but what Greenberg says elsewhere about the dating of the material must imply that any such work must have been done quite early, within the prophet's lifetime or very shortly afterwards. Greenberg would appear to rule out the much more long-drawn-out process of revision and expansion envisaged by Zimmerli and others.

There are a number of scholars ready to espouse and defend the holistic approach, but it must be stated that if holistic interpretation is seen as an attempt to side-step the critical and historical approach altogether it will take Old Testament scholarship into a dead end. The critical and historical questions may, with profit, be temporarily left aside while we explore other avenues, but they remain to be addressed. No interpretation of the final form of the text can ultimately avoid asking how that final form was achieved, since the way it has been arrived at is bound to affect its meaning for ourselves.

Alongside Greenberg's 'holistic' interpretation we may set the 'canonical' approach advocated by Brevard Childs, although Childs's methods can hardly be discussed in detail here, since they relate not only to Ezekiel but to the whole range of Scripture. Childs attempts to throw light on each book of the Bible by interpreting it in relation to its context in the canon, not only to the books and traditions which precede it but also to those that follow it. As far as Ezekiel is concerned, Childs, in his *Introduction to the Old Testament as Scripture*, tends to play down the historical specificity of the book. He stresses the book's *theological* interests in

60Ezekiel

such a way as to place them in some sort of opposition to its historical specificity. He says, for example, that, 'The book appears to lack the sharp contours of a given historical period, of a definite geographical locality, and of genuine prophetic preaching to a concrete group of listeners' (p. 357). A little later he tells us that, 'even when his oracles are fixed within a chronological framework, these temporal moorings are immediately transcended when the prophet describes the plan of God for Israel in terms completely freed from temporal limitation' (p. 361). Or again, 'when the prophet proclaims his message to the people, the historical addressee takes on such a highly theological profile that the concrete features of time and place fade into abstraction' (p. 362). On the following page we have, 'The effect of this theocratic concentration is that Ezekiel's message never takes on the particularity of the usual prophetic activity in which specific issues and groups are addressed in invective and threat'.

The first observation to be made is that none of these conclusions seems to depend on seeing Ezekiel in the context of the canon. It is hard to see how Childs's insistence on seeing the book in its canonical context has affected his interpretation at all here. The second observation is that I can only wonder whether Childs and I have been reading the same book of Ezekiel. As I hope to show elsewhere in this volume, the theology of the book of Ezekiel is rooted very specifically indeed in the precise situation of the exilic and early postexilic period. It addresses the issues *of that time*, and responds to the questions raised by the events of that period.

Like Greenberg, Childs himself by no means rejects or neglects critical methods, but the canonical approach, like the holistic one, lends itself to exploitation by those who wish to do exactly that. Both holistic interpretation and canonical criticism have shown that they can produce real insights in the hands of scholars who are well versed in traditional critical techniques. Whether they would be as fruitful in the hands of interpreters who had abandoned criticism altogether may be very seriously doubted.

One is left wondering whether both holistic interpretation and canonical criticism do not have, at their roots, a hidden agenda, by which their exponents, perhaps subconsciously, are seduced; and whether this agenda is not, in the last resort, implicitly fundamentalist. If so, then whatever the insights and achievements of these approaches might be, the approaches themselves must eventually prove inimical to scholarly method.

Further Reading

B.S. Childs, *Introduction to the Old Testament as Scripture* (London: SCM Press, 1979), pp. 355-57.

R.E. Clements, 'The Ezekiel Tradition: Prophecy in a Time of Crisis', in R. Coggins, A. Phillips and M. Knibb (eds.), *Israel's Prophetic Tradition* (Cambridge: Cambridge University Press, 1982), pp. 119-36.

E.F. Davis, *Swallowing the Scroll: Textuality and the Dynamics of Discourse in Ezekiel's Prophecy* (JSOTSup, 78; Bible and Literature Series, 21; Sheffield: Almond Press, 1989).

O. Eissfeldt, *The Old Testament: An Introduction* (Oxford: Basil Blackwell, 1965), pp. 365-82.

G. Fohrer, *Die Hauptprobleme des Buches Ezechiel* (BZAW, 72; Berlin: deGruyter, 1952).

—*Introduction to the Old Testament* (London: SCM Press, 1970), pp. 403-15.

J. Garscha, *Studien zum Ezekielbuch: Eine redaktionsgeschichtliche Untersuchung von Ezekiel 1–39* (Bern: Peter Lang, 1974).

H. Graf Reventlow, *Wächter über Israel: Ezechiel und seine Tradition* (BZAW, 82; Berlin: deGruyter, 1962).

M. Greenberg, *Ezekiel*, I (AB; Garden City, NY: Doubleday, 1983).

—'The Vision of Jerusalem in Ezekiel 8–11: A Holistic Interpretation', in J.L. Crenshaw and S. Sandmel (eds.), *The Divine Helmsman, Festschrift L.H. Silberman* (New York: Ktav, 1980), pp. 143-64.

F.L. Hossfeld, *Untersuchungen zu Komposition und Theologie des Ezekielbuches* (Würzburg: Echter Verlag, 1977).

A. Weiser, *Introduction to the Old Testament* (London: Darton, Longman & Todd, 1961), pp. 222-30.

W. Zimmerli, 'The Special Form- and Traditio-Historical Character of Ezekiel', *VT* 15 (1965), pp. 515-27.

—*Ezekiel* (2 vols.; Philadelphia: Fortress Press, 1979).

—*I am Yahweh* (Atlanta, GA: John Knox, 1982).

A collection of essays and papers giving a good indication of some of the new directions in which Ezekiel studies are moving is offered in J. Lust (ed.), *Ezekiel and his Book* (Leuven: Leuven University Press, 1986).

6

THE DATING SERIES

IT IS PROFITABLE to spend some time examining the series of dates which forms a kind of backbone to the book of Ezekiel. The details of this may well seem tedious but are worth some attention, since the series may give us some important clues about how the book has taken shape, and the authenticity of the dates has been a crucial issue in much critical discussion. When we wish to understand a prophetic saying or oracle it is usually helpful to know when the prophet uttered it, and in what circumstances. Sometimes this information is simply not available, and we are reduced to guessing. Sometimes it can be deduced (with a greater or lesser degree of certainty) from the content of the saying itself. Occasionally, the context in which the saying appears offers us information about the setting in which it was delivered.

In the book of Ezekiel, unusually, some of the material is explicitly dated, and these dates form an integrated series. Though the book is unusual in this respect, it is not unique. The dating of *individual* oracles or events (that is, the inclusion of dates but not as a series) is found also in the books of Isaiah and Jeremiah (see Isa. 6.1; 7.1; 14.28). These examples from Isaiah offer much vaguer dates than Ezekiel's, specifying only the year (6.1; 14.28) or, even more broadly, setting the event described 'in the days of Ahaz' (7.1). In the book of Jeremiah dates occur more frequently, but are for the most part no more precise. They, too, tend to specify only the year (1.2; 25.1; 32.1; 36.11; 45.1) or 'the beginning of the reign of' a particular king (26.1; 27.1; 49.34). Occasionally the month is specified (28.1; 36.9; 41.1). Zimmerli suggests that some of the Jeremiah dates may have been introduced at the editorial stage from narrative material in Kings.

Neither in Isaiah nor Jeremiah are dates used in the systematic way that we observe in the book of Ezekiel. The closer parallels are in postexilic prophecy. Both the book of Haggai and the first half of Zechariah contain precisely dated series of oracles, though in neither case does the series cover such an extensive period as in Ezekiel. Zechariah's dated prophecies fall within a span of two years, while those of Haggai cover no more than a few months.

The interest in precise dating may be more characteristic of priestly circles than of prophetic ones. It is certainly exhibited in the work of the Priestly school, notably in the Priestly version of the story of the flood.

Most of Ezekiel's dates fall within a seven-year period, though the last to be mentioned (in 40.1) is 14 years later than the latest of this main group, and the date listed eighth (29.17), which is out of chronological sequence, is two years later still.

Before considering the series of dates, we should note the reference in Ezek. 1.1 to 'the thirtieth year'. This is not part of the series. (The dates in the series are given in quite a different format.) Its interpretation is very uncertain and constitutes quite a separate problem. The number has been explained in a great variety of ways, as referring to (1) the prophet's age; (2) the year of King Jehoiachin's age (this is reckoned from 615 BC, and would have the effect of altering the year referred to in Ezek. 1.1 to 586 instead of 593); (3) the year of the current Jubilee cycle; (4) the year of the neo-Babylonian empire; (5) the period since the discovery of Josiah's Law Book.

Some suggestions only interpret the date by emending it. It has been said to refer to (6) the regnal year of Nebuchadnezzar (changing 'thirtieth' to 'thirteenth'), or (7) the year of Jehoiachin's exile (reading 'fifth' for 'thirtieth', in line with the following verse). The date has also been understood as referring to (8) the date of the book's completion (556 BC).

None of these suggestions has commanded general assent, but the one which seems currently to meet most favour is the first in the above list, that it refers to Ezekiel's age.

The main series consists of 14 other dates, given according

to the number of years after the deportation of King Jehoiachin, that is, after 597. They normally specify the year, the month and the day of the month, although one or two are incomplete. The earliest (1.1-2) is in the fifth year after the deportation, that is, 592, and the last of the main group is given as in the eleventh year, that is, 586. The final two (40.1 and 29.17) are considerably later, in the 25th and 27th years respectively.

It would be unwise to assume that, even where the dates are not defective, we necessarily have them in the form in which they were set down by the book's final editor. The textual evidence, especially of the Septuagint, shows that variants arose quite readily.

The series is as follows:

		Year	Month	Day
1.	Ezek. 1.1	5	4	5
2.	3.16 ('seven days later')	5	4	12
3.	8.1	6	6	5
4.	20.1	7	5	10
5.	24.1	9	10	10
6.	26.1 (month omitted)	11	?	1
7.	29.1	10	10	12
8.	29.17	27	1	1
9.	30.20	11	1	7
10.	31.1	11	3	1
11.	32.1	12^1	12	1
12.	32.17 (month omitted)	12	?	15
13.	33.21	12^2	10	5
14.	40.1	25	7 (?)	10

A number of problems arise. First, as already mentioned, some dates appear to be incomplete or defective. Secondly, it will be observed that the series is a not entirely tidy one: some dates are out of sequence. Thirdly, it is not clear how much of

1. Some commentators read '11th year', with some MSS of the Septuagint. This reading puts the oracles against Pharaoh in chronological order.
2. Again '11th year' is read by some scholars, following some MSS of the Septuagint and the Peshitta. This agrees better with the date of Jerusalem's fall as given in Kings and Jeremiah.

the material that follows each date is actually related to it. Do we assume that everything in the book that follows (let us say) date no. 4, relates to that date, until we get to date no. 5? Let us examine these problems in a little more detail. The apparently defective dates are three, that is, those in 26.1, 32.17 and 40.1. In none of these is the month specified in the usual way. In 32.17, though the Hebrew text simply omits any mention of the month, the Septuagint text reads, 'In the first month'. It may be that the Greek translators had a better Hebrew text in front of them, which contained the full date, but most commentators doubt this. It is quite likely that the Greek translators, like us, were faced with a gap in the text, and chose to fill it with something that made sense to them. If the Septuagint *is* correct, the date is out of sequence following 32.1 (the first day of the twelfth month), though the Septuagint itself keeps the sequence correct by reading 'eleventh month' in 32.1. In order not to be out of sequence the only month possible in 32.17 would be 'twelfth'.

40.1 is unusual. It reads, 'In the 25th year of our exile, at the beginning of the year, on the tenth day of the month, in the 14th year after the city had fallen...' Note, first, that we have here a *double* indication of date. Not only is the time specified, as in the rest of the series, by numbering the years since 597, the first deportation; it is also specified as 14 years after the *second* deportation, that is, after 586.

Furthermore, instead of designating the month by number in its usual way, the text reads, 'At the beginning of the year' (RSV translation). The Hebrew phase is *berôš haššānâ*, which in later Hebrew, at least, is the name of the Jewish New Year, which is in the seventh month. The status of the seventh month as the beginning of the year is determined by an older calendar than the one normally used in the book of Ezekiel. All the other dates are given according to what was then a fairly new system to the Jews, one derived from Babylon. In this postexilic system the months were designated by numbers and the year regarded as beginning in spring. Here, for once, the book reverts to the older calendar, which saw the year as beginning in autumn. The writer has not, therefore, omitted the month, but merely chosen to indicate it differently. The

Greek translators misunderstood this. They rendered the phrase *berôš haššānâ* as 'in the first month', thus bringing it into line with the book's normal usage, and overlooking the fact that in 40.1 the writer has momentarily changed calendars. The reason for the Hebrew text's phrasing is not difficult to deduce. Lev. 25.9 determines the year of Jubilee should begin on the tenth day of the seventh month. The vision which begins in Ezekiel 40 is dated at the very mid-point of a Jubilee period, reckoned from the beginning of the first captivity: it is being seen as half-way towards the hoped-for great year of release. The anomaly of the date in 40.1 thus turns out not to be due to scribal error, but to be of considerable significance for our understanding of the message of the text. The remaining defective date, in 26.1, really is simply a scribal error of omission.

Of more moment is the question of the dates which are out of sequence. The one most strikingly displaced is date eight, in 29.17, which relates to an oracle delivered in 'the 27th year', that is, in the year 571. This makes it the latest date in the series, though it stands eighth out of fourteen. The oracle which directly follows speaks of a campaign by Nebuchadnezzar against Tyre, which, it is implied, was unsuccessful. There is independent evidence (in Josephus, who cites earlier authorities) of a very long (13-year) siege of Tyre by the Babylonians, which, it can be calculated, must have ended shortly before 571. The date of Ezekiel's oracle may thus be said to be confirmed, so the fact that it stands eighth in the series calls for explanation.

Other anomalies are that the sixth date (in 26.1) in the eleventh year stands before the seventh date (29.1) in the tenth year. Chronologically, this sixth date should clearly come later in the series, but since it now contains no note of the month (see above), we do not know precisely where it should be placed in relation to dates nine and ten (30.20 and 31.1), which are also in the eleventh year.

Dates eleven, twelve and thirteen (32.1; 32.17; and 33.21), all in the twelfth year, also raise problems. Date eleven specifies the twelfth month, date thirteen the tenth, and the one which comes between, date twelve, is defective and contains no note of the month at all. The chronological sequence is thus manifestly incorrect, but the textual shortcomings of 32.17 ensure that we do not know what the correct one would be.

Date thirteen (33.21) has problems of its own. It appears to accord badly with dates given in Jeremiah and in 2 Kings. Jer. 39.1-2 (cf. 52.4-7) dates the breaching of the wall of the city in the eleventh year of Zedekiah, on the ninth of the fourth month. 2 Kgs 25.8 says that in the nineteenth year of King Nebuchadnezzar, he 'came to Jerusalem and burned the house of the Lord...' on the tenth of the fifth month. Ezek. 33.21, as the MT stands, appears to place the arrival of the messenger some eighteen months after the city's fall as dated by Kings and Jeremiah.

There is some support in the Septuagint, Peshitta and one or two manuscripts for reading 'eleventh year' in Ezek. 33.21. This is probably a scribal correction to bring the text more closely into line with 2 Kings and Jeremiah, though both Eichrodt and Zimmerli in their commentaries argue that the reading 'eleventh year' is original.

There may in fact be no discrepancy at all. Ezekiel, Jeremiah and 2 Kings all number the months according to the Babylonian system, beginning in spring; but it has been suggested that whoever was responsible for the dates in 2 Kgs 25.8 and Jer. 39.1-2 might still have been reckoning the years as beginning in autumn, according to the older system. This might account for the apparent difference of a year. Kutsch has an alternative explanation, that the year 598–97 was counted in Ezekiel as the first year of exile, which makes the years of exile one less than the regnal years of Zedekiah. If either of these explanations is correct, it would mean that we would then need to allow about six months for the messenger to reach Babylon. Given that according to Ezra 7.9 Ezra's journey from Babylonia to Jerusalem took four months, this does not seem unbelievable.

All of these out-of-sequence dates relate to oracles against foreign nations, and the easiest explanation of the present arrangement is that if they *were* originally in chronological order, they have been reorganized according to their subject

matter. Six of the seven blocks of oracles against foreign
nations are concerned with Egypt. The block beginning with
date six (26.1) consists of three whole chapters of elaborate
oracular material directed against Tyre. If it were placed in its
correct chronological position (wherever, precisely, that
should be in relation to dates nine and ten) it would interrupt
the oracles against Egypt. The anomalous date eight in 29.17,
prophesying that since Nebuchadnezzar has failed to subdue
Tyre he will be allowed to take over Egypt instead, certainly
looks more logical near the beginning of the series, after the
oracles against Tyre, but before the bulk of the prophecies
against Egypt, though perhaps a more thoroughly rigorous
logic would have placed it before the anti-Egypt oracle associated with date seven (29.1) rather than after it.

We can make sense of the whole existing series of dates if we
think of it as *two* series. First, there is a series concerned with
the prophet's activities and teachings relating to his own
people, which still stands in chronological order. This is represented by dates one to five, plus thirteen and fourteen. But this
series has embedded in it another series, concerned with
foreign nations (dates six to twelve), which have been
organized, or reorganized, in such a way as to take more
account of subject matter than of chronology.

This brings us to the third question regarding the dates: to
how much of the material following it is each date intended to
refer?

It has been observed that each date is followed—though not
always *immediately* followed—by material related to specific
events, that is, by oracles addressed to specific situations, or by
accounts of very particular prophetic enactments or visions.
Thus the date in 1.1-2 introduces the vision that marks
Ezekiel's call. The date in 8.1 is followed by chs. 8–11
describing the experience in which he felt himself transported
to Jerusalem. The date in 20.1 relates to an occasion when
'certain of the elders of Israel' formally consulted the prophet.
(The fact that the details given now make it rather uncertain
what they consulted him about does not belie the statement
that it was a matter of great particularity.) The date in 24.1
introduces enactments and speeches on the day when the

Babylonian siege of Jerusalem began.

The date in 3.16 is not immediately followed by anything so directly related to specific events, but by a brief anticipation of Ezekiel's 'watchman' parable (3.16b-21), which appears at greater length in ch. 33, and an even briefer mention of a vision like the call vision (3.22-24a). The specific actions to which the date seems to refer do not occur until chs. 4–5. They are introduced by the account of the prophet's dumbness (3.24b-27). The intervening passage thus seems to be composed of two pieces which echo material from elsewhere in the book.

In other instances passages of more general teaching are appended *after* the more specific material, and in a number of cases these more general passages have their own separate, undated, introductions. Such separate introductions encourage us to regard the passages following them as separate units. For example, ch. 13 is introduced simply by, 'The word of the Lord came to me' (cf. 12.17, 21, 26; 14.2; 15.1 and 16.1).

It makes sense of all these features if we suggest that the dates originally applied to the specific passages anchored to specific events or circumstances, or to sayings or actions relating to specific situations, and that the passages of more general teaching have been inserted into the series, usually at the end of the original dated unit, but in at least one case (at 3.16) breaking the connection between the date and the passage to which it was originally attached.

The one passage which does not fit the theory outlined above is 12.1-16 (or perhaps 12.1-20), which is not dated, but which is nevertheless highly specific, describing a symbolic action undertaken by the prophet as a prediction of the siege of Jerusalem. It is conceivable that this once *was* a dated passage, which has lost its date at some stage through editorial activity or scribal error. Alternatively, it may have been displaced, and have originally belonged with the little clutch of symbolic actions described in chs. 4–5.

In the foregoing analysis all the examples have been taken from the dated series of passages concerned with Judah and Jerusalem, but a parallel set of observations could be made were we to examine instead the series of passages concerning foreign nations. It looks as if in this case also the dated series was originally of sayings related to specific historical events or situations, such as Nebuchadnezzar's unsuccessful siege of Tyre (29.17-21), but that more general oracles against foreign nations, such as the collection of 30.1-19, have been interspersed.

If the analysis above is accepted, then we can complete our table of dates by adding a designation of the passage to which, it seems, each date is likely originally to have applied, together with a brief indication of its contents.

		Year	Month	Day		
1. Ezek. 1.1		5	4	5	1.1–3.15	Call vision
2.	3.16a	5	4	12	3.16a + 3.24b –5.17 or possibly 3.22–5.17	Three enacted prophecies representing the fate of Jerusalem
3.	8.1	6	6	5	chs. 8–11	The prophet's visionary trip to Jerusalem and the departure of the glory
4.	20.1	7	5	10	ch. 20	An enquiry by the Elders of Israel
5.	24.1	9	10	10	ch. 24	Prophetic enactments and speeches on the day the siege began
6.	26.1	11	?	1	ch. 26	Prophecy on Tyre's gloating
7.	29.1	10	10	12	29.1-16	Prophecy against Pharaoh
8.	29.17	27	1	1	29.17-21	Promise to Nebuchadnezzar that he will conquer Egypt

7

THE THEOLOGY
OF EZEKIEL

THE PHRASE 'THEOLOGY OF EZEKIEL' is ambiguous. Do we
mean by it 'the theology of Ezekiel the man', or 'the theology of
the *book* of Ezekiel'?

In fact, we must begin by speaking of the theology of the
book. The book is an existing artefact, about whose theology we
can make firm and checkable statements. And it does, as will
be shown, offer us a theology which is, in the main, coherent
and consistent, and which makes sense in the historical context to which it ostensibly relates.

How this theology which is discernible in the book relates to
the theology of the man Ezekiel is a much more hazardous
question to answer. The answer which any particular student
of the book gives will depend on how much of the book he or
she concludes may be ascribed to the activity of traditors and
editors and even copyists subsequent to the prophet's own
time. My own judgment is that the coherence of the book's
theology is such that it is likely, at least in its main outlines, to
reflect the single mind of an original prophet. Among present-
day scholars this view is shared by not a few. It remains, of
course, possible that the single mind which has imposed
coherence on the work has been an editorial one.

The Theology of Ezekiel in its Historical Context

Theology is never produced in a vacuum. The theology of the
prophetic literature, especially, is a response to a situation in
which the literature was shaped. The book of Ezekiel embodies

a response to the events of the beginning of the sixth century BCE.

This remains true even if considerable parts of the book do not derive from Ezekiel himself. Unless we date the book to some period radically different from the one to which it appears to relate (which only a very small handful of scholars have ever wished to do), then the book of Ezekiel, together with its postulated layers of expansion and interpretation, arises out of the exilic situation, and addresses the problems raised by the events of the early sixth century. Its theology makes excellent sense in that context, and indeed, is most readily understandable as an attempt to make sense *of* that context. The events of the early sixth century constituted a threat, the most serious which the people of Judah had had to face hitherto. Unless the dates given to us in the book are entirely misleading, Ezekiel did not begin his prophesying until he found himself in Babylon after 597. The first of the two blows that brought about the Judaean exile had already fallen. A substantial part of the material in the first half of the book seems to relate to this situation, in which the prophet asserts that more, and worse, is to come. Worse *was* to come, and in 586 Jerusalem again fell, and more of its citizens were deported; but this time Judah lost its temple, the focus of its national as well as religious life, and was no longer to be ruled by a king of the House of David.

The book of Ezekiel was produced by people who saw it as their job, in the face of all this, still to 'assert eternal providence, and justify the ways of God to men'. Of course, a not inconsiderable part of the Old Testament is devoted to the task of making sense of these events; of explaining why the exile happened, why it had to happen. But the core of the book of Ezekiel represents the work of one who lived through these events, and who was trying to make sense of what happened *as* it happened; and probably even the first layers of expansion of the Ezekiel tradition were produced by people who were still trying to cope with the effects of exile in their own lives.

The book of Ezekiel is an attempt to make sense of the exile, but not in the rather detached way that the academic historian 'makes sense' of such events. For Ezekiel's generation and Jeremiah's generation, 'making sense', *some* sort of sense, was a prerequisite of their own survival. As individuals, they had lost everything, except for what a man might put in a bundle on his shoulder and carry out in the dark. As a nation, they had lost everything that they thought of as essential to their nationhood: king, temple, independence; and above all, they had lost their land. They no longer had a place where they belonged.

The book of Ezekiel is produced by people trying to cope with this enormous sense of loss. And their survival is at stake because their identity is at stake. They have lost most of what defined them. What have they left that tells them who they are? In the Ezekiel literature they are still defined by their relation to a place, even though it is a place they have lost. And they are defined by their history, albeit a history which is throughout a history of failure. And they are defined, above all, by a grace that will not let them go, however much they themselves have deserved to be abandoned.

The Babylonian threat had not been unheralded. Prophets had already given warning of it, and had interpreted it in advance as divine judgment. Certainly Jeremiah had done so, though there were plenty of alternative prophetic voices who delivered a more reassuring message. The threat also had its precursor in the Assyrian imperial expansion towards the end of the eighth century. This Assyrian assault had eventually destroyed the Northern Kingdom, but had in the last resort left Judah, though subjugated, intact. The importance of this earlier eighth-century experience can hardly be over-estimated. It too had been seen by the prophets of the time as an act of divine judgment, and as a warning to Samaria's sister kingdom, Judah. Paul Joyce observes that in the Assyrian crisis prophecy 'sharpened the tools' which it was later to use in the Babylonian crisis. Jeremiah, at the end of the seventh century, and, in his turn, Ezekiel, at the beginning of the sixth, picked up these tools and wielded them effectively.

The warning constituted by Samaria's fall had been made all the more dire by the course of subsequent events. The monarchy of the Northern Kingdom had never been re-established. The nation's independence had never been

regained. And those who had been deported 'beyond
Damascus' never returned. The exiles of the North must
simply have been assimilated to the surrounding peoples and
lost their identity as Israelites. No Judaeans needed to be
under any illusions; this was what *could* happen if their land
was overrun by a foreign conqueror.

However, this interpretation of the events of 722 had not by
any means gone unchallenged. That the fall of Samaria and
the exile of the Northerners represented God's judgment on
the Northern Kingdom was not disputed. But whereas the
classical prophets saw this as a warning to Judah, there were
evidently others who, on the contrary, found reassurance in
it. They found reassurance in the fact that Jerusalem did *not*
fall to the Assyrians; its sanctuary was not destroyed; its king
was not deposed; and the people of Judah were not exiled.
However much Judah and Jerusalem suffered at the time, the
people retained their nationhood, their king, their cult. It was
possible, therefore, to take comfort from the thought that
Judah was either less wicked than Samaria or more favoured
by God. God evidently had Judah's interests more closely at
heart, and a better fate in store for it.

Those who argued thus evidently claimed prophetic
support. Isaiah of Jerusalem seems to have been credited with
having preached the inviolability of Zion. (We need not here
discuss with what justification the claim was made.) And the
events surrounding Sennacherib's assault on Jerusalem were
interpreted as providing evidence to reinforce this doctrine.
These events have been much debated, and the exact reconstruction of what happened is still problematical; but it is certain that, whatever the course of events may have been,
Jerusalem did not fall to the Assyrians. That, to some, was the
most significant fact, and from it they drew the reassuring
conclusion that God would at all costs and at all events defend
his Holy City and his sanctuary and the people of his covenant.
What seemed so clear to some of the prophets about the events
of the eighth century was, then, by no means obvious to many
of their contemporaries.

The same may be said of the events of 597. To Jeremiah, the
exile of 597 was the beginning of the final disaster, long

predicted by him and by others. Ezekiel, who of course did not begin his prophesying until after 597, saw it in the same way. But many of Jeremiah's and Ezekiel's compatriots evidently did not see it in that way. Eichrodt has drawn attention to features of the exile of 597 which must have made it look to the Jews far from final. They had, by the standards of the times, been let off lightly. They were still ruled by a native king (though a Babylonian appointee). And, perhaps most significantly, the deposed king Jehoiachin had not been dishonoured, but was housed in Babylon in a manner appropriate to his rank. (Contrast this with the fate of Zedekiah after 586. See Jer. 52.7-11.) The rest of the exiles seem also to have had a reasonable amount of freedom, and to have been able not only to support but to organize themselves and to sustain some kind of community life. This apparent lack of finality in the arrangements was seen by the Jewish community at large as grounds for hope. The exile, they anticipated, was likely to be short-lived. By the prophets Jeremiah and Ezekiel, however, this lack of finality was interpreted much more ominously. If the doom of 597 was not complete, this did not mean that it was only a temporary setback; rather, it was unfinished business. Much of the material in the first half of the book of Ezekiel, therefore, is devoted to demonstrating that the final judgment is still to come. However, once he had been proved right by events, and the blow of 586 had fallen, Ezekiel, like Jeremiah, devoted himself to asserting that even beyond that finality there was hope. Much of the rest of the book is designed to elaborate that hope.

The book's theology thus has two foci: the inevitability and irrevocability of judgment, and the awful totality of judgment, on the one hand, and yet on the other, the conviction that judgment was survivable, and that God *meant* his people to survive it.

It was largely due to the influence of the prophets that Judah did survive exile, and did not lose itself as the people of Samaria had been lost. As a badly injured person may, by an act of his or her own will, decide whether to let go or to go on fighting to live, so Judah, battered almost beyond belief, decided that it was not necessary to die. That it did so decide must be

placed largely to the credit of the prophets, of whom Ezekiel, at
this time, was a principal spokesman.

History, Judgment and Hope

One of the most crucial features of the book's theology is its
reshaping of history. It is clear from Hos. 2.14-15 (MT 2.16-17)
and Jer. 2.2 that there had existed a version of Israel's history
which saw it as having begun with a 'honeymoon period' (this
is precisely the language which Hosea and Jeremiah use) in
which Israel had been faithful to God and the relationship
between the two had been idyllic. This account of the history
survives only in Hosea's and Jeremiah's allusions. In our
existing records it has been replaced entirely by a much more
negative one. During the exile this more negative view evidently became the standard one, for it controls the presentation of the wilderness period which we now find in the
Pentateuch. Whether it originated in the Ezekiel tradition, or
whether the Ezekiel tradition simply appropriated an interpretation worked out by others, we do not know.

The book of Ezekiel comes back again and again to this
redrawing of history. It is set out most plainly in ch. 20.
According to this chapter, the Israelites provoked the Lord
even before leaving Egypt by their attachment to Egyptian
idols (20.6-8), and continued to provoke him by refusing to
obey the laws he gave them, especially the Sabbath law (20.10-
13). The second generation in the wilderness, in spite of divine
entreaty, was equally disobedient (20.18-21). After entry into
the promised land their derelictions continued, for they turned
to Baal worship, including child sacrifice (20.27-31). At every
stage the Lord thought seriously about destroying them, but
refrained from doing so, not because they deserved any
mercy, but simply 'for the sake of his name'. We are left in no
doubt that a totally black picture is being presented. At no
stage did the people respond favourably to God, or show any
inclination to obey him, or display any gratitude for what he
had done for them.

A similar interpretation of Israel's history is offered, though
in figurative form, in the extended parables of chs. 16 and 23.

In ch. 16 we have the parable of the foundling, which pictures Israel as an abandoned new-born baby. The Lord rescued her, brought her up, gave her everything, and eventually married her. But she was repeatedly unfaithful to him. It is strongly emphasized that, from the very beginning, the girl never had anything to commend her. She is of alien parentage (16.2-3), so there are no ties of blood to give her any claim on her finder's charity. When the Lord first encountered her she was repulsive and filthy, and it is implied that she had already been rejected and abandoned as worthless by her natural parents (16.4-5). Though she does later become very attractive the text stresses that this was due entirely to the care and expense that the Lord lavished upon her (16.9-14). Her only reaction was to exploit the gifts which the Lord had given her, in order to engage in harlotry and idolatry (16.15-34). We have here the same heavy stress as in ch. 20 on Israel's total unworthiness, total lack of response, total and repeated failure of gratitude.

In ch. 23, the story of Oholah and Oholibah, the two kingdoms of Judah and Samaria are separately represented by the two wives in a polygamous marriage. The text briefly mentions that the sexual adventures of the two began in Egypt, but the parable concentrates mainly on later phases of the history. However, even this brief mention (23.1-3) establishes the point that sexual licence was characteristic of the pair from their earliest nubility. (The text alludes again to the Egyptian experience in 23.19-21.) Oholah (Samaria) is accused of harlotry with the Assyrians 'while she was mine', that is, while she was actually married to the Lord. She is severely punished for this (a reference, of course, to the events of 722). Oholibah (Jerusalem) takes no warning from her sister's example, but likewise engages in harlotry, first with the Assyrians and then with the Chaldaeans.

The parable thus complements and extends the parable of the foundling. It traces the history of unfaithfulness into the period of the kingdoms, and its reading of that history is as thoroughly negative as anything in chs. 20 or 16. The two women characters are presented as being without redeeming features. Their one interest is sexual promiscuity and at no stage do they show any loyalty to their husband. When we put together the evidence of these three chapters, 16, 20 and 23, the picture is unmistakably consistent. The negative evaluation of Israel's history is emphatic, even laboured. It must be repeated that this negative evaluation is not unique to the book of Ezekiel. The Pentateuchal traditions as they have come down to us are structured around a series of 'murmurings' in the wilderness, and of various acts on Israel's part, which, where they are not acts of outright rebellion, are at least expressions of serious lack of confidence in the God who had saved it. As far as Israel's subsequent history is concerned, its presentation in the work of the Deuteronomic historians stresses the nation's inveterate tendency to slide into idolatry and its leaders' frequently exhibited propensity to do 'that which was evil in the eyes of the Lord'.

But while the picture offered in the book of Ezekiel is not unique in being negative, it is uniquely black. Israel in the wilderness, according to the Pentateuchal traditions, was not *altogether* unreceptive to divine instruction, and there is nothing in the Pentateuch corresponding to Ezekiel's accusation that even before they left Egypt Israel remained impenitently attached to Egyptian gods. Likewise, in the Deuteronomic historians' picture of the post-settlement Israel, the nation's tendency to slip into apostasy is at least partly counterbalanced by the work of a series of leaders who keep dragging it back onto the path of loyalty.

The stress in the book of Ezekiel on Israel's unworthiness to be chosen has its counterpart in Deuteronomy, for example in such texts as Deut. 7.6-8. But the same text does go on to assert positively that, nevertheless, 'the Lord set his love upon you and chose you'. The passages in Ezekiel which we have just considered make no comparable assertion. Not only are they remarkably insistent that Israel had no virtue, and nothing attractive about it to prompt the Lord's interest, but they are surprisingly silent about what God's motives *were* in initiating the relationship at all. The origins of the Lord's interest in Israel are in the book of Ezekiel left totally unexplained.

It must be noted, however, that though a totally black picture of the *past* is being presented, there is no such pessimism about the future. In 20.33-44 the return from exile is pictured, and pictured as a second exodus, which, unlike the former exodus, will lead to a successful outcome. It will include the same elements as the former experience, a 'bringing out' from among the nations, a leading through the wilderness, confrontation in the wilderness, and consequent purging of the rebellious elements, and at last the bringing to the holy mountain, where sacrifices will be offered—though the holy mountain, this time, is not Sinai but Zion.

How does this interpretation of history *function* in relation to the theology of the book? It is doubly important, for it relates to both halves of the book's message: it provides the foundation both of the certainty of judgment and for the hope of salvation. It explains the destruction of Jerusalem and the exile by prompting the rhetorical question, 'What else could we expect?' (the Deuteronomic interpretation of history, though less gloomy, does exactly the same). But the Ezekiel interpretation of history also provides the foundation for hope, because if, in the past, even the most relentless failure of response on the part of Israel did not prevent God from preserving the relationship 'for the sake of his name', then there is no reason why he should be prevented now. If Israel's continued existence rests simply and solely on divine grace, with not an atom of a possibility that the nation deserves it, then all that means is that it rests where it has always rested. Israel has nothing to commend it. It deserves nothing but destruction. If it is to have any future it will only be because God wills it, for *his* sake not for Israel's. So what is different? It was always so.

Such is the line of argument implicit in the book. When we thus explore the way in which it interprets, or reinterprets, the history and traditions of Israel, we perceive that the whole work is, in essence, an elaborate theodicy.

The Remnant, Judgment and Hope

Thoroughgoing pessimism about the endemically sinful condition of the nation would appear to leave little room for any belief in the existence of a righteous remnant. The book explicitly denies the possibility that there might be a remnant for whose sake the rest might be saved. According to Ezek. 14.12-20, 'even if these three men, Noah, Daniel and Job were in it' (that is, in the land) these persons of legendary virtue 'would deliver but their own lives by their righteousness'.

On the one hand this is a further expression of the totality of the corruption of the nation. Even the traditional and important prophetic office of intercession is devalued, as Jeremiah, with the same intention, had already devalued it (see Jer. 11.14, 14.11, 15.1). The nation is past praying for.

But the observation that the nation is, and always has been, totally unresponsive, leaves at least one member of it out of account, namely, the observer. Ezek. 14.12-20 assumes the possibility that the righteous few might at least save *themselves*. The thinking is similar to that expressed in Genesis 18, the story of Abraham's intercession for Sodom and Gomorrah, and the subsequent story of Lot in Genesis 19. There is no righteous remnant large enough to induce God to save the community from destruction, but one righteous person may nevertheless be saved *out of* the community. That the message of the nation's total depravity must leave out of the totality the one who delivers the message seems tacitly to be assumed in the passages referred to above. But the question is raised explicitly and addressed directly in the parable of the watchman. This is set out at length in ch. 33 and anticipated briefly in 3.16-21.

The watchman parable is necessary because the composer of the book is in danger of digging himself into a hole which will entomb his whole enterprise. If the situation is really as hopeless as it is being made out to be, why is he wasting his time? If there has never been any response from anybody, and there is never likely to be, why persist with the message? If the canvas is to be painted in unrelieved black, does it justify the painter's effort in producing the picture?

Just occasionally the book seems to allow that not quite all *is* unrelieved black. 9.3-9 envisages the possibility that there are 'those who sigh and groan over all the abominations committed' in the city, and who are marked out to be spared from destruction. Joyce, however, in his exegesis of this chapter (in *Divine Initiative and Human Response in Ezekiel*) notes that all the emphasis in Ezekiel 9 is on the totality of the destruction, and he takes the conversation in 9.8-10 as open to the interpretation that no such righteous persons were in fact found. (Cf. Ezek. 22.30, and also Jer. 5.1.) If there were any, they are not referred to elsewhere in the account of the vision. But whatever we say of 9.3-9, the book cannot exclude the remnant idea altogether. If everyone else fails, the prophet himself must assume the role. This is effectively what happens in the watchman parable, though the book itself does not express it in that way. The watchman's dilemma is that he knows no one will listen. If he *really* knows that, it must prompt the question, 'Then why keep watch? Why deliver the warning?' The answer given in the parable itself is in terms of responsibility. Given that the people are totally unresponsive, they will heed no warning. The consequent disaster will be their fault. But if, anticipating their unresponsiveness, the watchman does not *deliver* the warning, the disaster will be the same, but this time it will be *his* fault. This will hardly matter to the people, but it will matter to him.

There is a different kind of 'remnant' referred to in 14.21-23. These are the few who will survive the disaster. But they are emphatically not a *righteous* remnant and they do not survive because they deserve to. They function partly in the way the 'two legs or a piece of an ear' function in Amos 3.12, that is, as evidence that the disaster took place. But in ch. 14 this unrighteous remnant is more than evidence that the disaster happened—they are evidence that it was deserved, for by their continuing evil deeds they bear witness that the Lord's punishment was justified.

'Individual Responsibility'

All of this brings us to the subject of what has been called 'individual responsibility' in Ezekiel. Discussion of this centres on ch. 18. This chapter is in fact written to meet the problem which is raised by the very negative view of Israel's history which we find expressed in the book. The 'sour grapes' proverb which is quoted at the beginning of the chapter appears to be simply drawing the logical conclusion from the prophet's own interpretation of the history of the nation. If things really are as bad as chs. 16, 20 and 23 make them out to be, then the past shortcomings of the nation have made its downfall inevitable. The generation of the exile was quite entitled to reply, 'Then how can *our* repentance, for our small part of this vast tally of sin, make any difference, or be sufficient to avert divine wrath and the disaster which is its expression?' This is the question which ch. 18 sets out to answer.

Paul Joyce asserts, correctly in my view, that ch. 18 is not concerned with what has been called 'individual responsibility'. It is the moral responsibility of each *generation* for its own sins that is the point at issue. The writer of ch. 18 is thinking very firmly in terms of corporate guilt.

Joyce says that, 'Although a single man is considered in each of the three test cases, it is the cause of the *nation's* predicament which is being explored' (p. 46; my italics). He points to the contrast between the rule which had always (as far as we can tell) been applied in Israel's 'criminal law', that only the guilty party should be punished, and the notion of corporate guilt which seems generally to have applied in the religious sphere. (The principle that only the guilty party should be punished is *enunciated* in Deut. 24.16, but all Old Testament law is based on the assumption that it applied.)

The tension between the two seems to have been perceived. Joyce notes (p. 50) that in the work of the Deuteronomic school itself this tension seems to be unresolved. Individual responsibility is asserted in Deut. 24.15, but in the Deuteronomic interpretation of history corporate responsibility is assumed.

Joyce points out that Ezekiel 18 is concerned with two logically distinct questions:

1.   For whose sins is the exile a punishment—those of the prophet's own generation, or those of their forebears? His audience, he assumes, think that they are being punished for their ancestors' sins (which is the point of the 'sour grapes' proverb). Ezekiel's argument is designed to show that it is their own sins for which they are being punished.

2. There is the question of repentance. They *are* sinners, but repentance will atone for all.

Joyce notes that as far as the first question is concerned, Ezekiel uses a legal argument in which legal and theological assumptions run in parallel. Both in criminal law and, on Ezekiel's interpretation, in the economy of God, people are not punished for other people's wrong-doing. But when it comes to the argument about repentance, human law and the divine economy do *not* go hand in hand. In law, not only is a person of hitherto good character held responsible if he or she lapses and commits an offence, but an offender who is penitent and turns over a new leaf is still held responsible for the offences he or she has committed. At this point, legal and theological principles diverge. The crucial verse is 18.23: '"Have I any pleasure in the death of the wicked?" says the Lord, "and not rather that he should turn from his way and live?"'

Ezekiel is at this point no longer thinking in terms of what has misleadingly been called 'Israel's criminal law', but in terms of *family* law. If one is thinking of the law administered by magistrates and judges, then the idea that the penitent offender should go unpunished seems unthinkable; but if one is thinking in terms of the authority wielded by the *paterfamilias* over his household, such an idea is much more easily credited. Ezekiel may be thinking of a legal situation such as that presupposed in Deut. 21.18-21, the Law of the Rebellious Son. In such a situation as that described in Deuteronomy 21 a parent would, surely, seize on *any* evidence of a genuine change of heart as a reason for not carrying out the sentence.

Sin and Expiation: Judgment and Hope

It will be of value if at this point we look in more detail at what is understood in the book of Ezekiel by 'sin'. If we look at the nature of the specific sins denounced in the book, we find them to be, to a large extent, the same as those denounced in earlier prophecy. The *social* sins mentioned are broadly the same as those condemned by Amos and Isaiah. (See, for example, the diatribe against the 'shepherds' in Ezek. 34.)

In the sphere of religion, the book catalogues the same old offences of idolatry and apostasy as did Ezekiel's predecessors (see, for instance, ch. 8). The forms of idolatry vary a little from generation to generation, but the basic accusation remains the same. Where the book of Ezekiel varies the traditional prophetic catalogue is in laying emphasis on Sabbath-keeping and on offences against purity regulations, such as engaging in sexual intercourse when a woman is menstruating.

It is important to observe that although for our own purposes we distinguish between 'social' sins and 'religious' ones, the book itself does not do so. What seems to us a logical distinction was either not perceived as such by those responsible for the book's production, or, more probably, was not regarded as important. There are, for example, various catalogues of sins in chs. 18 and 22 in which social and religious offences are mixed in what looks like an entirely random way.

Where the Ezekiel tradition differs markedly from earlier prophetic literature is not in the sins specified, but in the language in which they are spoken of. The book uses for preference the priestly/cultic language of defilement. The people's offences are repeatedly described as 'abominations' (*tôʿēbôt*). *tôʿēbâ* signifies 'that which fills one with revulsion and disgust'. It is not an exclusively priestly/cultic word (it is not uncommon, for instance, in the book of Proverbs), but it is predominantly so. It appears once in Isaiah (1.13) where in an ironic statement incense is described as a *tôʿēbâ* (incense was generally regarded, of course, as a delight to the Lord). Jeremiah uses the word in a handful of cases; other prophetic literature before Ezekiel's time does not use it at all. In the book of Ezekiel the word occurs some 40 times. There is no question, therefore, but that among the prophetic books, the word is highly characteristic of Ezekiel.

The book also makes great use of the word 'to profane' (*ḥālal*). 'To profane' is the opposite of 'to hallow', 'to make holy', 'to keep holy'. It speaks, for example, of profaning the Sabbaths; always—speaking in Yahweh's name—called '*my* Sabbaths' (20.16, 21; 22.8; 23.38). It also speaks of profaning the sanctuary (23.39; 24.21; 44.7). Once, in a striking phrase, we have the Lord saying, 'You have profaned *me*' (13.19). But most frequently, the book speaks of profaning the *name* of Yahweh (20.14, 22, 39; 36.20, 21, 22, 23).

What all this 'abomination', 'uncleanness' and 'profanation' demands is cleansing, purification and expiation. This is most often spoken of in ritual and religious terms, but not exclusively so. 22.17-22 talks of purifying, and burning out corruption, but in the imagery of the metal refinery. Compare the image of the cauldron in Ezek. 24.1-14. This begins as a picture of the stew pot (the besieged city) in which the meat (its citizens) are to be seethed. But at some stage in the development of the tradition this has been overlaid with a parallel picture of the pot so contaminated with decaying matter and corrosion that it can only be cleansed by setting it dry upon the fire until the contamination is burnt away.

Alongside the language of defilement goes the language of rebellion. The people are frequently referred to as a 'rebellious house' (some 15 times). The adjective used is $m^e r\hat{\imath}$, a cognate of the word employed in Deut. 21.18-21 to describe one who rejects parental authority.

The language of uncleanness and that of rebellion seem at first sight unrelated, but there is more of a connection between them than might appear. What is 'abominable' is so because it offends God: 'rebellion' is that which fails to pay due regard to his honour and his authority. Both 'abomination' and 'rebellion', therefore, indicate a failure of respect, a failure to recognize the divine holiness and its demands. A passage which well illustrates the association between the two sets of ideas is Numbers 16 (MT 16.1–17.15). It does not actually use either of the words 'abomination' and 'rebellion', but it does relate the two areas of thought. The account is the complex one of the fate of Korah, Dathan and Abiram. The offence of these three is a rebellious act. It involves a challenge to Moses' authority and to the prerogatives of the sons of Aaron. But it is actually expressed in a cultic act, the offering of incense. Now the offering of incense can be a powerfully efficacious expiatory ritual, as the passage itself illustrates (Num. 16.41-50; MT 17.6-15); but in the wrong hands it becomes grossly offensive—so grossly offensive as to merit an exemplary punishment unparalleled in Scripture. What is ritually or religiously inappropriate, if engaged in knowingly and with set purpose, is at the same time both an abomination in God's eyes (though again it must be noted that the passage from Numbers does not use the word) and an act of rebellion. (That unauthorized persons trespassing on areas or activities reserved for priests should be put to death is stated in Num. 3.10, 38; 18.7.)

It is perhaps not insignificant that the account of the offence of Korah, Dathan and Abiram in Numbers 16 follows closely, though not immediately, on the passage in Numbers 15 about sins 'with a high hand', and may, together with the story in Num. 15.32-36, about the man who gathered sticks on the Sabbath, be intended as an illustration of what the phrase 'sin with a high hand' might mean. The complex in Numbers 15–16, concerned as it is largely with priestly prerogatives, is likely to emanate from exactly the kind of priestly circles whose traditions have so powerfully influenced the book of Ezekiel.

Along with the characteristic way of speaking about sin as 'abomination' and defilement goes a characteristic emphasis on grace mediated through purification and expiation. Along with this goes a very positive attitude to the temple and its cult, and this positive evaluation of the temple and its ritual is an integral part of the theology with which the book presents us.

The attitude of the prophets before Ezekiel's time to the temple and to sacrifice is one that has been much debated. Certainly the pre-exilic prophetic literature contains some very critical assessments of the cult, though it is not always clear how radical these are intended to be. Ezekiel's contemporary Jeremiah, if the book that bears his name is reliable on this point, took a more negative view of the temple than most. Whatever problems of interpretation arise in appraising the attitudes to the temple of Ezekiel's predecessors, one thing is quite clear: none of them gives the temple an important part in his thinking, and ideas of cultic purity and sacrificial expiation are not central to their understanding of God and the way he deals with humanity.

In the book of Ezekiel these themes *are* central. Sin, as we have seen, is consistently spoken of in the language of the cult, in terms of ritual purity; and the idea of ritual expiation of sin is taken seriously. Above all, the temple is important as the place where the presence of God properly dwells. This importance of the temple is brought out most strongly in chs. 40–48. These last nine chapters of the book have sometimes been judged not to be derived from Ezekiel himself but to be a later addition to the tradition. However, as the book stands, they are certainly integrated into its structure. Central to these chapters is the description of how 'the glory of the Lord' returns to the Jerusalem sanctuary (43.1-5). This is the glory which the prophet is pictured as encountering in Babylonia (ch. 1). He beholds the glory again on his 'flying visit' to Jerusalem in chs. 9–11. In 43.1-5 the glory of the Lord returns permanently to his place.

The temple is certainly not *exclusively* the place where God can be met. Ezekiel 1 makes the point emphatically that his presence can be encountered wherever his people happen to be. Nevertheless, Jerusalem with its temple is the place which is *appointed* for meeting God, and the return of the 'glory' to Jerusalem is a sign that normality has been restored, and that God's relationship with his people has once more been regularized.

The expiatory system is important in the scheme of things because, if history teaches that Israel has been totally unresponsive in the past, it would clearly be rash to assume that it will be totally responsive in the future. If Israel's past is one of unrelieved failure, then provision must be made for handling failures to come.

On the subject of sin, the prophetic tradition up to Ezekiel's time had thought itself into something of an impasse. Though the eighth-century prophets constantly appeal for repentance they frequently express scepticism about the likelihood that repentance will be shown. Amos, in particular, appears to be extremely pessimistic about this. All the pre-exilic prophets seem to be convinced of the inevitability of judgment. If they speak of restoration, then implicitly or explicitly it is generally clear that they envisage it as being *beyond* judgment. There may be hope *after* judgment has done its work and brought

Israel to its senses. For the pre-exilic prophets the answer to sin is punishment, and if punishment fails to produce repentance they really have nothing else to suggest. This is the dilemma that is expressed so baldly in Amos 4.6-12, a passage which contemplates the possibility that, since lesser disciplinary disasters have not had the desired effect, only the final judgment is left.

The book of Hosea has a great deal to say about judgment, but it does seem to contain the perception that what is seen as sin and disobedience arises from the failure of a relationship, and a lack of response to which judgment by itself does not provide a satisfactory answer. In the book of Hosea there is an unresolved tension between two convictions, the conviction that final judgment is the only answer, and the conviction that final judgment is no answer at all, that it is inconsistent with the ultimate purposes and character of God. We can get rid of this tension, perhaps, by taking the book apart, or by assigning the two conflicting views to different phases of the prophet's career. Such suggestions have certainly been made. But this is the easy option, and simply disembowels the book's theology. Any solution which resolves the tension between judgment and hope is untrue to the book, because that tension is what the book is about.

Isaiah of Jerusalem finds a partial answer to the dilemma with his notion of the remnant. The remnant idea allows for the possibility of thoroughgoing judgment, and yet allows hope beyond it.

In Jeremiah the tension that we see in Hosea becomes, if anything, even more acute. At one point he seems explicitly to reject the remnant idea as a solution. (See Jer. 5.1-5, especially 5.1, though see also, by contrast, the parable of the good and bad figs in ch. 24.) The book of Jeremiah is full of images which convey the idea that sin is endemic, ingrained. It is rooted in defects of character which cannot simply be removed by exhortation or threats of punishment. Israel is, in a sense, genuinely helpless against its sin, because it proceeds from a corruption of the will itself. Such is the depth of depravity that it can be answered only by a remaking of the personality, a remaking of the will. This is the point of the language about the 'new heart' in Jer. 31.31ff. Whether this radical hope is a realistic hope is another question altogether. What is striking is that in all this earlier prophetic literature nowhere is the cult or the expiatory system seen as offering any real answer to the problem of dealing with sin. What is original about the Ezekiel tradition is that it does countenance this possibility. Indeed, the stone that Jeremiah and the rest rejected is in Ezekiel made the head of the corner.

Further Reading

P.R. Ackroyd, *Exile and Restoration* (London: SCM Press, 1968), pp. 103-17.

P. Joyce, *Divine Initiative and Human Response in Ezekiel* (JSOTSup, 51; Sheffield: JSOT Press, 1989).

K. Koch, *The Prophets*, II (London: SCM Press), pp. 84-118.

T. Krüger, *Geschichtskonzepte im Ezechielbuch* (BZAW, 180; Berlin: deGruyter, 1989).

J.D. Levenson, *Theology of the Program of Restoration of Ezekiel 40–48* (HSM, 10; Missoula, MT: Scholar's Press, 1976).

B. Lindars, 'Ezekiel and Individual Responsibility', *VT* 15 (1965), pp. 452-67.

J. Lindblom, *Prophecy in Ancient Israel* (Oxford: Basil Blackwell, 1962).

G. von Rad, *Old Testament Theology*, II (Edinburgh: Oliver & Boyd, 1965), pp. 220-37.

W. Zimmerli, 'The Message of the Prophet Ezekiel', *Int* 23 (1969), pp. 131-57.

8

THE BOOK OF EZEKIEL AND OTHER PROPHETIC TRADITIONS

OUR EXAMINATION OF THE STRUCTURE and characteristics of the book of Ezekiel has already raised the question of Ezekiel's relationship to both earlier and later prophecy. It will be useful to pursue this topic further; this will involve summarizing some of what has already been said.

K.W. Carley in his book *Ezekiel among the Prophets* has explored very thoroughly the similarities between Ezekiel and the pre-classical prophets. Much of what follows is based on Carley's work.

1. The motif of 'the hand of the Lord' is found in Ezek. 1.3; 3.14, 22; 8.1; 33.22; 37.1 and 40.1. Most of Carley's parallels from earlier tradition are not in fact from prophetic literature. The examples offered by earlier prophecy are 1 Kgs 18.46; 2 Kgs 3.15, and Jer. 15.17. Isa. 8.11 is also a possible example.

2. The motif of the 'Spirit'. 'Spirit' language also appears in accounts of the pre-literary prophets. Clear examples are 1 Sam. 10.6, 1 Kgs 18.12 and 1 Kings 22 (see especially 1 Kgs 22.21-24). Carley notes that when Ezekiel uses the word *rûaḥ* it is not always explicitly the spirit of God or of Yahweh which is referred to. In fact the phrases *rûaḥ ᵉlōhîm* and *rûaḥ yhwh* are rare in Ezekiel. The book often uses the word *rûaḥ* without the article. Carley further observes that the Spirit motif drops out of use in the eighth-century prophets. Only in Hosea and Micah are traces of the motif still discernible. See Mic. 3.8 ('I am filled with power by the spirit of the Lord') and Hos. 9.7, which parallels *nābî'* with *'îš hārûaḥ* ('man of the spirit').

3. The phenomenon of translocation, at the instigation of the Spirit. 1 Kgs 18.12 and 2 Kgs 2.16 postulate this phenomenon of Elijah. Ezekiel speaks of being 'lifted up' or 'brought' by the Spirit in 3.12, 14; 8.3; 11.1, 24; 43.5.

4. Carley sees a connecting link between Ezekiel and earlier prophecy in the prominence given to the theme of divine self-justification. He is building here on the work of Zimmerli, for whom a key passage is 1 Kings 20. At four points in the narrative of 1 Kings 20 an oracle is delivered which is provided with a reason justifying it: 1 Kgs 20.28, 'Because the Assyrians have said...therefore I will give all this great multitude into your hand'; 1 Kgs 20.36, 'Because you have not obeyed...Behold...a lion shall kill you'; 1 Kgs 20.42, 'Because you have let go...your life will go for his life...'; 1 Kgs 20.13 is similar, except that the causal language is implicit rather than explicit: 'Have you seen all this great multitude? Behold I will give it into your hand...'

Zimmerli sees this as an ancient oracular pattern, and observes that in Ezekiel the two-part formula recurs frequently, though by Ezekiel's time it had begun to break down to some extent. It occurs especially in the oracles against foreign nations: Ezek. 25.3-5; 25.6-7; 25.8-11; 25.15-17; 26.2-6; 29.6b-9a; 35.5-9 and so on.

In two of the examples in 1 Kings 20, vv. 13 and 28, an extra clause is added: 'and you shall know that I am the Lord'. This last phrase (or phrases which are its close equivalents) is very characteristic of Ezekiel.

If Zimmerli is right, then there is indeed a striking similarity between the book of Ezekiel and pre-classical prophetic tradition. Fohrer, however, has criticized Zimmerli's argument, and sees the 'And you shall know...' formula in 1 Kgs 20.13 and 28 as a late insertion, dependent on Ezekiel's own work. Von Rad regards the formula 'See, I am giving it into your hand', which also appears in 1 Kgs 20.13 and 28, as not specifically prophetic at all. He takes it to be rooted in the tradition of the Holy War, and sees it as the sort of formula used in oracles delivered before a battle, not only by prophets but by priests.

The form-critical argument, therefore, must be judged

inconclusive. And if we look at the broad theme of divine self-justification or self-demonstration it must be said that it occurs quite widely, and is not confined to prophetic material. The theme is explicit, for example, in Exod. 6.1-8, which contains, at v. 7, the precise words 'and you shall know that I am the Lord your God...' It underlies Exod. 20.2, Deut. 5.6 and Ps. 81.10 (MT 81.11). Compare Jer. 9.24 (MT 9.23).

It may also be observed that the phrase 'I am the Lord your God', though without the added 'and you shall know...', appears repeatedly in a priestly/legal context in Leviticus 17–19 (especially ch. 19). But although in Leviticus 17–19 the phrase 'I am the Lord' may properly be said to express divine self-demonstration, Yahweh's authority and divinity is not here something which emerges from the demonstration of his mighty acts, in the manner of a conclusion to be drawn, as it is in the other examples quoted above. Rather, it is asserted as the ground and motivation of Israel's obedience to the law.

Nevertheless, it is interesting to find the book of Ezekiel echoing so closely a characteristic expression of the Holiness code. In its emphasis on the theme of divine self-demonstration, therefore, it looks as if the book of Ezekiel is drawing on a spectrum of earlier traditions, probably including both prophetic and priestly ones.

5. Carley also observes, alongside the theme of *divine* self-justification or self-authentication, the theme of *prophetic* self-justification. He finds this prominent in both Ezekiel and Jeremiah and connects this with the prominence in both books of autobiographical prose, noting that it is primarily in autobiographical prose materials that the prophet defends or asserts the authenticity of his own inspiration.

The necessity for authentic prophecy to prove itself in the face of dissent and opposition is perhaps best seen as an inevitable feature of prophecy in any age. It is certainly very prominent in Jeremiah, where it is a component not only of Jeremiah's struggles with false prophecy, but also of his struggle with self-doubt. But it is by no means lacking at earlier stages of prophecy. It is the central theme of 1 Kings 22 (the story of Micaiah) to say nothing of 1 Kings 18 (Elijah on

Carmel). It emerges strongly in Amos 7.10-17 (Amos's argument with Amaziah).

Carley notes that the ultimate criterion of true prophecy is the fulfilment of predictions, and that this is stressed both in Deut. 18.22 and Jer. 28.9. Carley also suggests that the *dating* of prophecies may have the same purpose, of offering evidence of accurate and genuine prediction. In fact dated prophecies are hardly found at all in prophecy before Ezekiel. The closest we come to it is in Isa. 8.1-2. The giving of prophetic names to children may sometimes have had the same purpose, since the age of the child would offer an indication of date to the prophet's contemporaries. Isa. 8.14-17 and 8.3-4 are the most obviously relevant texts here.

6. Carley sees Ezek. 4.4-8 as evidence of the idea of prophetic suffering for the sins of others. Ezekiel's lying on his side for periods of 390 days and 40 days signifies that the Lord 'will lay the punishment of the house of Israel upon [him]'. 'You shall bear their punishment', he says. Carley does not claim that this idea draws on earlier prophetic tradition, though Exod. 32.30-34 might be quoted. The idea of vicarious suffering is, of course, developed in Deutero-Isaiah, especially in Isa. 52.13–53.12, though whether this and other 'servant' passages refer to a *prophetic* figure is disputed.

Dependence on Jeremiah

We have already noted some similarities between Ezekiel and Jeremiah in our general consideration of Ezekiel's connections with earlier prophecy. There are some points, however, not previously noted, at which the Ezekiel tradition's dependence on Jeremiah is quite marked.

The book of Ezekiel often elaborates what in Jeremiah are little more than hints, or brief metaphors, and builds them up into something much larger in scale. It has often been observed that the effect is as if Ezekiel were preaching sermons on Jeremiah's texts. For example: Ezekiel 18 seems to be taking as its jumping-off point Jer. 31.29-30, both quoting the 'sour grapes' proverb; Ezekiel's refusal to mourn for his wife (see especially 24.16) might be seen as an expansion of

Jer. 16.5; Ezekiel 37, the vision of the valley of dry bones, may
have arisen out of a meditation on Jer. 8.1-3, and Ezekiel 23
looks very much like a 'sermon' on Jer. 3.6-11.
But the most striking example is Ezekiel's imagery of the
new heart in 36.26-27, prefigured in 11.19. This idea occurs, in
an undeveloped form, in Jer. 24.7 and 32.39, and the Ezekiel
passages also recall Jer. 31.33, the 'new covenant' prophecy.
Here Jeremiah, though he speaks of the law being 'written
upon their hearts', does not actually speak of a *new* heart, but
it is noteworthy that in both Ezek. 11.20 and 36.28 statements
about the new heart are followed immediately by the covenant
formula, exactly as in Jeremiah 31. The thinking in the
Ezekiel passages and in Jeremiah 31 is running on closely
parallel lines.

The theme of the new heart is not confined to Jeremiah and
Ezekiel. It is found also in Ps. 51.10 (MT 51.12), where, as in
Ezek. 11.19 and 36.26-27, the new heart is paralleled by a
'new spirit'. It is not possible to be certain whether Psalm 51
pre-dates or post-dates the book of Ezekiel.

Dependence on Hosea

The specific associations between Ezekiel and Hosea are less
striking than those between Ezekiel and Jeremiah, but are not
to be overlooked.

Ezekiel 16 and 23 certainly develop, and at length, the
'unfaithful wife' theme so prominent in Hosea. We must reg-
ister the fact, however, that virtually every major prophetic
book picks up this theme at some point, albeit in some cases
very briefly. For instance, compare Isa. 1.21; 50.1; Jer. 2.33–
3.5; cf. 2.20-25.

As was mentioned above, the clearest antecedent of Ezekiel's
parable of Oholah and Oholibah is to be found in Jer. 3.6-11.
But it may be easier to see the influence of Hosea in the parable
of the foundling in Ezekiel 16, for here, in a considerable literary *tour de force*, Ezekiel actually fuses *both* of Hosea's great
images, that of Israel the unfaithful wife and Israel the rebellious and ungrateful child.

While on the subject of the foundling parable, it has been

claimed by Gese that Ezekiel is here echoing a tradition according to which Yahweh 'found' Israel in the wilderness. This is also said to be echoed not only in Hos. 9.10 (and perhaps 10.11), but also in Deut. 32.10, Jer. 2.2-3 and 31.2-3. Finally, it is claimed that Ezek. 20.33-44, which speaks of the new exodus, echoes Hos. 2.14-15 (MT 2.16-17). However, the Ezekiel passage presents the wilderness experience primarily as an experience of judgment, whereas Hosea envisages it as an experience of restoration and new beginning, a 'second honeymoon'. There is no real parallel here.

I have so far spoken as if similarities between the book of Ezekiel and words ascribed to earlier prophets could only be explained on the assuption that Ezekiel or the compilers of the book that bears his name were influenced by these ostensibly earlier traditions. It remains possible, however, that the prophetic books have at some stage been edited together as a single corpus, and that linking themes and images have been introduced or emphasized during that editorial process.

Ezekiel and Later Prophecy

The book of Ezekiel is typical of later prophecy in the following respects:

1. The difference between the style of Ezekiel's visions and that of earlier prophecy has already been noted. Instead of terse and impressionistic descriptions we have what are often quite elaborate narratives. The content of the visions is sometimes given in great detail and the images often have an element of strangeness, tending even to the bizarre. These features appear in prophecy after Ezekiel's time, notably in Zech. 1.7–6.8, and later still in apocalyptic writing. Another notable feature of Ezekiel's visions is the presence in many of them of a heavenly interpreter, who explains to the prophet the vision's significance. This heavenly interpreter is also prominent in the Zechariah passage and in apocalyptic writing.

2. Ezekiel's interest in legal matters surfaces again in later prophecy, notably in Hag. 2.10-14. Alongside this goes an interest in the cult and a positive evaluation given to the

temple and its sacrificial and festal system. The best illustration of this in later prophecy is in Mal. 1.6–2.16.

3. The phenomenon of translocation, which we have seen to connect with earlier prophecy, also hints at later developments. It seems to link with a feature common in apocalyptic writing, namely, the visionary journey, in which the seer is taken on a sort of spiritual 'conducted tour'. The best-known example of this is in *1 Enoch* (chs. 17–36). The story of Elijah's being taken up to heaven (2 Kgs 2.11) may offer a jumping-off point in earlier tradition for this idea.

4. Finally, the use of dated prophecies has already been noted as a feature which connects Ezekiel with Haggai and Zechariah.

Further Reading

K.W. Carley, *Ezekiel among the Prophets* (London: SCM Press, 1975).
W. Zimmerli, *Ezekiel*, I, pp. 42-46.

9

THE FINAL VISION: EZEKIEL 40–48

THOSE WHO HAVE FOUND the priestly elements in Ezekiel uncongenial, or have seen them as difficult to reconcile with the prophetic, have shown a tendency to devalue the last nine chapters of the book as a sort of appendix, or even to challenge the authenticity of this section, regarding it as no true part of the message of the original prophet. A good case can be made out, however, for seeing it as the book's climax.

The material of these chapters is at first sight quite different in kind from the rest of the book. The chapters contain long lists of measurements of the temple, and a good deal of material of a legal sort, mostly concerned with the cult, the ordering of festivals and sacrifices and the duties of priests, and also with the apportionment of land. But we must not lose sight of the fact that all this is set in the context of a vision, not unlike that of chs. 8–11. In both visions the prophet is supernaturally transported to Jerusalem and has a view of the city (8.2-3; 40.1-2). The former vision concludes with an account of how the prophet was returned to his place of exile in Babylonia (11.24). The vision of chs. 40–48 has no such ending.

Before analysing these chapters further, it will be useful to summarize, in order, their content.

Outline of Contents of Ezekiel 40–48

The section begins, as noted earlier, with a date, a double date in fact: in the 14th year after the fall of Jerusalem and the 25th after the first deportation.

40.1-4 describes the circumstances of the vision. The prophet is brought by the hand of God, in visions, to Israel, and set down 'on a very high mountain', from where he sees 'a structure like a city', which turns out to be the temple. A 'man', 'whose appearance was like bronze', introduces himself. His function is to explain what the prophet is seeing.

40.6–42.20 consists of a series of measurements of the temple, made by Ezekiel's guide.

43.1-12 describes the return of the divine glory to the temple. The prophet is ordered (by a voice from within the sanctuary) to convey to Israel the instructions for the building of the temple and for the conduct of its worship. (This theme of the divine glory which takes up its residence in the temple may be paralleled in Exod. 40.34ff. and 1 Kgs 8.10ff. Compare also Isa. 6.3ff.)

43.13-27 gives regulations concerning the structure of the altar of burnt offering.

44.1-3 returns to the subject of the divine glory. The eastern gate, by which the glory re-entered, is to be closed for ever to human thoroughfaring.

44.4-27 details rules governing who shall be allowed into the sanctuary, and ordinances concerning the life and functions of the temple's personnel.

44.28-31 details the priests' emoluments.

45.1-9 explains that land around the temple is to be allocated for the support and sustenance of the priests, the Levites, the rest of the population and the prince, with advice to princes not to oppress their people.

45.10-17 lists rules concerning the provision of regular sacrificial offerings.

45.18-25 lists regulations concerning sacrifices for the major cultic occasions of the year.

46.1-15 lists rules for the organization of worship.

46.16-18 lists rules concerning the property of the prince.

46.19-24 returns to a description of the temple, or at least part of it, the kitchen area.

47.1-12 contains a vision of the river flowing out from the temple, widening and deepening as it flows.

47.13-20 contains a description of the boundaries of the land.

47.21–48.29 details how the land of Israel is to be divided among the tribes, with the temple lands, land for the population of Jerusalem, and for the prince, in the middle of it. (This picks up the subject of 45.1-9.)

48.30-35 indicates the extent of the city and enumerates its gates.

The overall pattern of these chapters is thus a somewhat untidy one. Similar subjects are not all dealt with in the same place. For example, 47.21–48.29 looks as if it belongs logically with 45.1-9; and 46.19-24 would look more in keeping with 40.6–42.20. It seems as if a basic vision of a restored temple in the midst of a restored community has been filled out with material spelling out some of the precise regulations governing life in this new age.

Having summarized the material in the order in which it is presented, let us now try to classify it according to subject matter. The subject matter of chs. 40–48, as will be observed from the foregoing outline, mostly resolves itself into five principal topics. These topics are not mutually exclusive, and to some extent overlap. Moreover, as already observed, the material on each topic is not all placed together in one section. The topics are:

1. The account of the vision itself, which includes the details of the plan of the restored temple, and of the return of the glory of the Lord. The description of the temple (at least) appears to have been filled out and expanded. For instance, 46.19-24, the description of the kitchens, is not connected to the rest.

2. The regulations concerning sacrifices and other aspects of worship: mostly in 45.10–46.15.

3. The temple personnel, priests, Levites, their functions and some rules governing them: mostly in 44.5-31.

4. Allocation of the land and description of its boundaries: 47.13-20; 47.21–48.29; cf. 45.1-9 (allocation of land in the vicinity of Jerusalem and of the sanctuary area).

5. Regulations relating to the prince, his functions, his obligations and his property: 44.1-3; 45.7-8; 48.21-22.

Information about the duties of the prince is also interspersed in the sacrificial legislation of 45.13–46.18.

Before going further, it is worth observing that this pattern of themes links the work of Ezekiel very strikingly with the work of Moses. The parallels are not exact, but are too remarkable to be ignored. Moses leads his people to worship at a 'very high mountain'. On the mountain he is given instructions about the building of a sanctuary (a tabernacle), with a detailed account of its form and measurements. Moses ordains a priesthood and give the priests instructions as to their duties; he gives divine instructions regarding the cult, its festivals and its sacrifices, and finally he surveys the land—though the division of it is left to his successor (Deut. 34). Only the regulations concerning the prince are missing from the Mosaic prefiguration.

Although at first sight, then, the last nine chapters of Ezekiel look quite different from the rest of the book, in some respects the themes of this section fit very well into the book's pattern. They are, in form, a vision of Jerusalem and its temple, in which the prophet is said to have been transported from Babylon to his homeland. They thus balance the earlier complex of chs. 8–11. Central to chs. 40–48 is the restoration to Jerusalem and its temple of the divine glory, the presence of the Lord. This glory appeared to the prophet in exile in ch. 1 and was seen again temporarily resident in the city when Ezekiel visited it in chs. 8–11; in 43.1-5 it returns permanently to its proper place. Looked at in this way these three great visions can be seen to form a major structural element of the book of Ezekiel.

There are other thematic linkages between the last nine chapters and the rest of the book. Levenson points out that the description of Zion as 'a very high mountain' in 40.2 is strongly reminiscent of the description in 17.22-23, which undoubtedly also refers to Zion (cf. 34.14).

Chapters 40–48 also fit well with the theme of ch. 20, where the goal of the new Exodus is seen as the offering of sacrifice on the holy mountain of Zion. It is in accordance with this that the end and climax of the book should be a vision of the restored temple and its restored cult.

In addition to all this, the themes developed in chs. 40–48 fit very well into the scheme of the book's theology. Central to its message is the threat of Jerusalem's capture and the destruction of its temple, and the abandonment of its regular worship. Much of the book turns around the dramatic fulfilment of that threat. What more natural than that when it turns to prophecies of hope, that hope should include the restoration of temple and cultus?

The priestly and sacral interests so evident here are not confined to the last nine chapters. The themes of these chapters are to a large extent developments and elaborations of ideas which can be shown to be present elsewhere. As we have seen, the thinking of the book is dominated by the problem of theodicy, raised in very sharp form by the exile and near-destruction of the nation, and by the question, 'How, if we ever *are* restored, can we prevent it all happening again?' The restoration of the temple as a place where sin can be atoned for, the careful protection of its sanctity and the equally careful regulation of what goes on in it, all help directly to meet the problem. In the light of this, therefore, it is not remarkable that the subject matter of chs. 40–48 should be covered in the book of Ezekiel.

But if it would be hasty to reject Ezekiel's authorship of the last nine chapters out of hand, it would also be hasty to assume uncritically that everything in them must be authentic writings of the prophet. If, as is widely believed, there has been a stage (or stages) in the development of the Ezekiel tradition at which priestly interests have made their mark, what more likely place than the final chapters of the book for such interests to make themselves felt? On analysis, it looks as if a considerable amount of such priestly material, much of it of a programmatic kind, has been worked into the book. Much of the classic work on the analysis of these chapters was done by H. Gese, whose principal work on the subject was published in 1957.

It seems likely that the earliest strata of the tradition did contain an account of an ecstatic vision, in which the prophet saw the restored Jerusalem and its temple, but that the content of this vision has been filled out at later stages, largely by people with a strong interest in regulating the postexilic cult. Some of this filling out presumably happened at a fairly early stage of the transmission of the material, before the forms of law which we now have in the Pentateuch had crystallized into their present state. At some points the laws in chs. 40–48 are inconsistent with Pentateuchal law (a fact which in the first century CE caused some embarrassment in rabbinic circles). It looks as if the legal/cultic material in these chapters may correspond to what in British parliamentary practice is called a 'white paper', that is, suggestions for reform which may later find their way into firm legislation, but only after revision and amendment.

The description of the temple which these chapters contain is by no means a complete one. It would not be possible to reconstruct from Ezekiel's description and measurements a picture of the building. What the book offers us is basically a ground plan with little indication of elevation, no mention of the materials of which the temple is to be made and very little note of the nature of its decoration or interior furnishings. It is not clear to what extent the description mirrors that of Solomon's temple, of which Ezekiel's generation would still have had clear memories, and how far it represents idealized (or stylized) proposals for a newly conceived replacement. It is possible that the description of the temple in Ezekiel 40–48 bears the same sort of relation to the real Second Temple as the cultic/legal material of the book bears to the laws in the Pentateuch, that is, it may have been a kind of draft plan which was open to modification in the light of further discussion (and perhaps in the light of what the community could afford).

Further Reading

H. Gese, *Der Verfassungsentwurf des Ezechiel (Kap. 40–48) traditions-geschichtlich Untersucht* (Tübingen: Mohr, 1957).

J.D. Levenson, *Theology of the Program of Restoration of Ezekiel 40–48* (Cambridge, MA: Harvard University Press, 1976).

10

MESSIANISM IN THE BOOK OF EZEKIEL

ONLY A SMALL NUMBER of passages are relevant here, for on any showing the figure of the messiah is not prominent in the book of Ezekiel. 21.25-27 (MT 21.30-32) has sometimes been considered to be a messianic oracle. It is an obscure passage, but recent opinion, following an article by Moran in 1958, is that the verses are best understood as a judgment oracle. Moran argues that the messianic interpretation depends on nothing more substantial than the fact that its phrasing recalls Gen. 49.10 (the 'Shiloh' oracle—another obscure passage which has traditionally been seen as messianic). We can safely dismiss Ezek. 21.25-27 from consideration.

More relevant is 17.22-24. These verses are set in the context of, and conclude, the curious allegory of the great eagle. The allegory itself is contained in 17.1-10, and, in the context of the exilic period, it has a fairly obvious interpretation. An eagle breaks off a twig, which he carries away and transplants. This clearly represents Jehoiachin and the first wave of exiles. The eagle is Babylon. The tree left behind (Zedekiah and his supporters) flirts with a different eagle. The consequences, says the passage, will be disastrous. These verses seem to belong chronologically in the period between 597 and 586.

There are close parallels between the allegory in Ezekiel 17 and Jothan's parable in Judg. 9.7-15 (cf. 2 Kgs 14.9). Verses 11-21 spell out this interpretation in some detail, though there are hints that the chronological perspective is different from that of the allegory itself, and that the interpretation, in its present form, has been influenced by the actual experience of the second deportation. Verses 22-24, which are the actual messianic verses, speak of another twig which will be planted 'on the mountain height of Israel', and which will grow to become a great tree. This oracle turns emphatically towards the future. It envisages a restoration to the homeland (the planting 'on the mountain height of Israel') and seems to be speaking of an ideal ruler who is to come. Verses 22-24 thus extend the thought of ch. 17 into new ground, though in an undeniably logical direction. Were they an original part of the allegory and its interpretation, or have they been added at a later stage? Opinions differ. 17.23 is strongly reminiscent of Dan. 4.10-12, 20-22, but this proves little as to date, since it is likely that both the author of Daniel and the originator of Ezek. 17.23 are drawing on the same mythological traditions, rather than one being dependent on the other. My own view is that vv. 22-24 look very like an afterthought which has no integral connection with the allegory itself.

The next passage to be considered is Ezek. 34.23-24. This too is set in the context of an allegory or parable, that about the shepherds. The passage begins with strong criticism of the 'shepherds', that is, the rulers of Israel. In 34.9-10 judgment is threatened against them. In vv. 11-16 the prophet announces that God himself will be the shepherd. Up to this point the image of flock and shepherd has been developed quite consistently; but in vv. 17-19 there is a new departure. The shepherds drop out of sight, and now it is the leaders of the flock itself, the leading sheep and goats, who are criticized. This is not consistent with the preceding verses and constitutes a different and alternative development of the image of the flock of Israel. Verses 20-22 pronounce judgment on these corrupt leaders and promise salvation from them for the flock.

Verses 23-24 introduce a new promise, that God will set up 'one shepherd, my servant David'. He says, 'I, the Lord, will be their God, and my servant David shall be prince (*nāśî*') among them'. This looks like an alternative to the promise of 34.11-16, that the Lord himself will be the shepherd. In vv. 23-24, the Lord is to be God; the shepherd will be an earthly ruler, 'David'.

The most natural explanation for what we find in ch. 34 is

that we have here an original parable, condemning the shepherds of Israel, and promising that God himself will shepherd them, to which have been added, firstly, vv. 17-19, which present an alternative development of the image of the flock, and secondly, vv. 23-24, which offer an alternative form of the promise of a good shepherd. It is not impossible that these developments were quite early. It is not inconceivable that the prophet himself might have used the same image and explored it in quite different ways at different times. But the messianic promise does look very like a development which has overlaid the primary interpretation.

It is perhaps worth remarking that there is a similar situation in ch. 37, the account of the vision of the valley of dry bones. There an original, clearly delineated image, that of an army of dismembered skeletons on the open plain which comes dramatically to life, has had added to it an interpretation (in 37.11-14) which uses the same basic notion of a resurrection, but pictures it as an opening of graves, in a manner quite inconsistent with the picture first drawn. This illustrates a phenomenon which is typical of the book of Ezekiel, that a coherent image or piece of teaching has laid alongside it a passage which has a similar point of departure, but understands and develops the basic thought in a significantly different way.

The final messianic passage is Ezek. 37.15-28. The context here is that of an enacted prophecy in which the prophet apparently takes two sticks (some interpret them as two trees, as if some sort of grafting operation were perhaps involved) and holds them together in such a way that they appear to be one. This prophesies the reunification of the two halves of the country. Verses 15-19 describe what the prophet was instructed to do; 20-23 concentrate on the *message* of the enactment. The interpretation contains the words (v. 22) 'and one king shall be king over them all' (the Septuagint seems to have read 'and one ruler shall be over them all'). There is then a third section (vv. 24-28) which speaks more explicitly in messianic language: 'my servant David shall be king over them; and they shall all have one shepherd' (v. 24; note the strong echo of 24.23) and 'David my servant shall be their prince (*nāśî'*) for ever' (v. 25). It is noteworthy that this third section, which speaks of David, makes no explicit reference at all back to the enacted prophecy.

The basic enacted prophecy, with its prediction of reunification, makes excellent sense in the context of Ezekiel's lifetime. The reunification of the country had been an issue since Josiah's time, and finds expression in Jeremiah (for example, Jer. 3.6ff. and chs. 30–31). The prophecy of a Davidic king suggests a post-586 perspective, when Israel had been deprived of its royal house. Zimmerli argues that, 'the unselfconscious use of the title "king" for the future ruler of the united country' suggests a date earlier than that of the passages where the title has been replaced by *nāśî'*.

My own suggestion would be the opposite, that it is more likely that the basic stratum of the Ezekiel tradition used the word *nāśî'* because it was more in line with political realism. Within the lifetime of the prophet the possibility of the restoration of the royal house must have looked remote. The possibility of a return, perhaps under the leadership of a native Israelite governor of non-royal status, was a far more realistic expectation. (As it happens, when return to Palestine did become a reality, after the conquest of Cyrus, this is precisely how it was done.) The use of the title 'king' seems to me to mark out the prophecies containing it as later additions to the traditions, emanating from an age when a messianic idealism had taken over, which took little account of political realities.

Conclusion

Leaving aside Ezek. 21.25-27 (MT 21.30-32), we have three passages in Ezekiel containing messianic predictions, in chs. 17, 34 and 37. In each case the messianic oracle looks like an addition, extending the thought of the basic passage, or developing it in ways that ignore, or are not totally consistent with, what seems to be the earliest stratum of tradition. In any one case it might be said that this conclusion is arguable, but the fact that all three passages exhibit a similar pattern strengthens the feeling that the messianic ideas present in the book have entered the Ezekiel tradition at a later stage of its development.

Further Reading

W.L. Moran, 'Genesis 49.10 and its Use in Ezekiel 21.32', *Biblica* 39 (1958), pp. 405-25.

11

THE *nāśî'* IN EZEKIEL

THE BOOK OF EZEKIEL makes a good deal of use of the word *nāśî'*, traditionally translated in the English Bible as 'prince'. In particular, it uses the word to describe the ruler of the restored state of Israel, to which the book looks forward. The question arises, why does the book use this particular word? Is it deliberately chosen in preference to the word 'king'? Or are there no such implications? Is it anticipated that the restored state of Israel will be headed by a king, or by some kind of non-royal ruler?

These questions are intertwined with the question of messianism, discussed above. Is the 'prince' seen in the book of Ezekiel simply as a ruler of the restored Israel in a mundane, perhaps medium-term future, after a return from exile; or is he in some passages viewed as a more messianic figure, in a more distant eschatological future?

Perhaps the most useful starting point is to ask what the word *nāśî'* normally means in biblical Hebrew. It occurs over 120 times in the Hebrew Bible, of which some 36 are in the book of Ezekiel. In the vast majority of instances the word occurs in narratives relating to the early period of Israel's history, or occasionally in the laws, and is applied to tribal leaders. It appears to be applied fairly widely, and not exclusively to the highest ranking leaders. In Num. 16.2 we have a gathering of 250 of them, and in several other cases the *nāśî'* is described as a head of a *bêt 'āb*, which is not normally thought of as a particularly large unit. In Numbers 13 all the men sent to spy out the land are said to be *nᵉśî'îm*. In Gen. 25.16 (cf. Gen. 17.20) *nāśî'* is used for heads of the Ishmaelite tribes. Hamor the Canaanite is called a *nāśî'* in Gen. 34.2, and Abraham is given the title by the Hittites in Gen. 23.6. In none of these instances is there any question of royal status.

Royal status *is* involved, however, in 1 Kgs 11.34, in Ahijah's prophecy to Jeroboam. Solomon's successor is to be deprived of his hegemony over the northern tribes, but he will remain as *nāśî'*. This *may* imply reduction of status, but there seems to be no suggestion that Solomon's successor will cease to be thought of as royalty.

We may conclude from all this that the word *nāśî'*, as used in the Hebrew Bible, is a general word meaning 'leader', which certainly does not imply royal status, but does not exclude it. That is to say, a *nāśî'* was not usually a king, but it was not felt inappropriate to apply the word to a king. It is noteworthy that the word appears most frequently in the priestly strata of the Pentateuch, in the work of the Chronicler, and in Ezekiel; that is, predominantly in literature of the exilic and postexilic period.

If we turn now to the way the word is used in the book of Ezekiel we find this picture broadly confirmed. The word is used on a number of occasions of Israel's leaders in general, usually in the plural: see Ezek. 7.27; 19.1 (here the Septuagint reads the singular. If this is correct the word *nāśî'* would refer to the reigning king); 21.17 (English versions 21.12); 22.6 (here the *nᵉśî'îm* could conceivably be a *succession* of kings rather than a group of contemporary leaders); 45.8, 9. In 7.27 we find, 'the king shall mourn, the prince shall be wrapped in despair'. If the two statements are to be taken in parallel, the king and the *nāśî'* are equated.

The word is applied in a very similar way to the leaders of foreign nations. Gog is described as 'chief prince', if that is a correct rendering of the phrase *nᵉśî' rôš* in 38.2, 3; 39.1. And 39.18 refers collectively to the 'princes of the earth' who are casualties in Gog's army. 26.16 speaks of the 'princes' of Tyre; cf. 27.21 (Kedar), 30.13 (Egypt) and 32.29 (Edom). So, as in the Hebrew Bible outside Ezekiel, the word is applied most frequently to persons of rank in Israel or other nations who are not necessarily, and demonstrably not usually, of royal status.

34.24 and 37.25, passages already considered, prophesy in

what are evidently eschatological contexts that 'my servant
David shall be *nāśî'* among them'. Whoever was responsible
for these passages manifestly did not feel that the word *nāśî'*
was inappropriate to apply to royalty and, equally obviously,
did not feel that to call a royal figure *n āśî'* implied any
diminution of his status. As we have seen, it may be that 34.24
and 37.25 belong to a late stratum of the tradition, so it is
important to observe that the use of the word *nāśî'* to designate
royalty is not confined to such passages. 21.30 (English
versions 21.25) refers to a particular *nāśî'*, whom it calls a
'vile, wicked prince of Israel'. Zimmerli comments that by this
'only Zedekiah can be meant'. Ezek. 12.10 and 12 also seem to
refer specifically to Zedekiah, and to the particular
circumstances of his attempted escape from the doomed city.
So when the book uses the word *nāśî'* in the context of the final
vision to refer to the political ruler of the restored Israel (44.3;
45.7, 16, 17, 22; 46.2, 4, 8, 10, 12, 16, 17, 18; 48.21, 22) it is
employing a term which seems to be a general word for
'leader' or 'ruler', which does not usually imply royal status,
but does not exclude it. In its range of meaning the word *nāśî'*
seems to be very close to the English word 'ruler'. An English
speaker could quite naturally use a phrase like 'our rulers',
and would be understood to mean the nation's political leaders,
the government, perhaps members of parliament. Yet a
sovereign or other head of state could properly be called a
'ruler', and would feel no insult in the designation. If we take
into account, therefore, the usage of the Hebrew Bible in
general, and that of the book of Ezekiel in particular, we see
that in his references to the leader of the restored Israel the
writer has chosen consistently to use a word which neither
implies nor denies royal status.

The most natural way to explain the choice of term is to see
it as quite deliberate. The writer has opted for a neutral word,
which in the circumstances of the time was the most appropriate thing to do. The restored community which is envisaged must necessarily have some sort of civil head, but at the
time when most of the material was being composed it must
have been wholly unclear whether Judah could realistically
expect to have a ruler with the status of king, or whether the

imperial power would keep a tighter hold by appointing a civil governor of non-royal rank. The writer may simply be leaving his options open, and defining the duties rather than the status of his envisaged head of state. It would not have needed a lot of imagination to visualize the possibility of a civil governor, since the Babylonians appointed Gedaliah to such a role after 586. And it is interesting to note that when the Jewish community *was* eventually restored (an event of which nothing in the book of Ezekiel reflects any knowledge) it was given exactly such leaders, first in the person of Sheshbazzar, and then, a little later, of Zerubbabel, and that Sheshbazzar is actually called *nāśî'* in Ezra 1.8.

Further Reading

W. Zimmerli, 'Plans for Rebuilding after the Catastrophe of 587', in *I am Yahweh* (Atlanta, GA: John Knox, 1982), pp. 111-33 (see especially pp. 123-25).

12

GOG AND MAGOG:
EZEKIEL 38–39

A NUMBER OF BASIC PROBLEMS arise with regard to these chapters. The first concerns their content. They are unlike anything else in prophecy up to the exilic period. Superficially, they may be said to resemble the oracles against foreign nations, with which the book of Ezekiel (and several other prophetic books) abounds. But closer examination shows that their style is distinct from the usual style of oracles against foreign nations. Furthermore, whoever put the book of Ezekiel into its present form has not placed them in the section of oracles against foreign nations, and evidently did not perceive them as belonging there.

They consist of oracles against a 'chief prince' Gog, who is threatening Israel, or is expected by the prophet to threaten it. The destruction of Gog and his armies is prophesied at some length. Who is this 'Gog' against whom these oracles are directed? Is he a historical character, and is the prophet speaking of an actual threat of military attack which his people faced, or which he anticipated they would face in the near future? Or is the prediction an eschatological one, and Gog a mythical figure?

There is another problem relating not to the nature of the chapters but to their position in the book. Why are they placed just here? At this point in the book the theme of judgment has been largely left behind and all is directed towards hope and restoration. Chapters 38–39 read very oddly after the promise of restoration which constitutes ch. 37.

This leads on to a further question: at what point have these

materials entered the Ezekiel tradition? Were they there in
the earliest stratum, perhaps going back to Ezekiel himself?
Are they eschatological, virtually apocalyptic material which
has been added later, when an interest in such things had
developed in Judaism? Or was the material there from an
early stage but only in embryo, having had its eschatological
and perhaps cosmic dimensions added to it by reinterpretation
as the tradition grew? Certain observations can be made at
once about the identity of Gog which limit the possible answers
to some of these questions. No one corresponding to Gog, and
no events or circumstances corresponding to the Gog threat,
have been satisfactorily identified in the Near East of the exilic
period.

Where, then, did the name 'Gog' originate? The range of
suggested explanations of the name is quite astonishing. Some
suggestions have been associated with attempts to date the
book of Ezekiel later than the exilic period. Gog has been
identified as an officer in the army of Cyrus the younger,
around 400 BC (Messel). He has been identified with
Alexander the Great (Torrey and Browne). Van den Born,
similarly, puts Gog in the Greek period, but sees the name as
originating in a misunderstanding of an abbreviation for the
Hebrew word for 'Macedonian'. Gog has been seen as a 'locust
giant' like the scorpion man of Mesopotamian mythology
(Gressmann). The name has been said to derive from the
Sumerian word *gûg*, 'darkness'. On this understanding Gog is
seen as darkness personified (Heinisch). Some see Magog as
the original name, and Gog as derived from it.

The word 'Gog' also has been seen as relating originally to
the name of a tribe in Asia Minor (Albright) or Northern
Assyria (Dürr). Albright adds the suggestion that the name
had come to mean 'barbarian'. The most probable explanation
of the name 'Gog' is that it is derived from that of Gyges of
Lydia, whose name appears in Assyrian annals as 'Gugu'.
This Gyges lived in the seventh century, and if the Gog
traditions are drawing on memories of Gyges, they are
drawing on a figure who seems already to have become
legendary before the period of Judah's exile.

The threat posed by Gog is not, therefore, a mundane, historical threat. The names of Gog's associates, Cush, Put, Gomer and Beth-Togarmah, are none of them names of historic or actual enemies of Israel. The same may be said of the lands of Meshech and Tubal, of which Gog himself is said to be 'prince'. Nor had the Persians, mentioned among Gog's associates in 38.5, emerged as a threat up to Ezekiel's lifetime. The names which can with any plausibility be assigned to specific geographical regions are mostly situated either in Asia Minor or the area just to the east of it. The exceptions are Persia (already mentioned), Cush and Put, which all occur in 38.5, a verse which may be part of a later expansion. This association of most of the names of Gog's companions with the general area of Asia Minor may strengthen the connection of 'Gog' with Gyges, whose kingdom was in Asia Minor. To an ancient Israelite this was 'the North', and such evidence as we have suggests that the Israelites' knowledge of this region was vague. To them, the North was in all probability the mysterious and threatening North, the home of strange and unknown people. It is perhaps best to conclude that the names of Gog and his associates are chosen precisely *because* they are foreign and mysterious.

It is more than likely that whoever originated the Gog oracles was taking his cue from Jeremiah. We have already noted how often it happens in the book of Ezekiel that ideas and themes which Jeremiah throws out, or briefly alludes to, are taken up and developed, sometimes at length. Thus Ezekiel's parable of Oholah and Oholibah in ch. 23 looks like an elaboration of Jer. 3.6-10, and the watchman parable, which appears in Ezekiel 3 and 33, may be derived from what is almost a throw-away line in Jer. 6.17. Similarly, Ezekiel 38–39 may readily be regarded as elaboration of Jeremiah's brief and cryptic prophecies about a 'foe from the North', whom he never names. See, mainly, Jeremiah 4–6, and especially 6.1ff., 6.22ff.; but compare also Jer. 4.11ff. and 5.15-17.

But the theme of the *destruction* of the 'foe from the north' is not present in Jeremiah. That appears to have its antecedents in the preaching of a still earlier prophet, Isaiah of Jerusalem. According to Isaiah, Assyria is the enemy whom

God has appointed to punish his people. Thus in Isa. 10.5ff. Assyria is the 'rod of my [i.e. Yahweh's] anger'; a stick with which to beat his people. But eventually, says the prophet, Assyria itself is to be punished (see for instance Isa. 10.12ff.; 10.15ff.; 10.24-27; and especially 14.24-27).

The names of Gog's allies, and the name Magog, which seems in Ezekiel 38–39 to designate the land from which he comes, appear to be derived from a tradition which surfaces elsewhere in Scripture in Genesis 10.

Before suggesting any further conclusions about the composition of these chapters, it may be useful to reproduce in summary Zimmerli's analysis of the passage. This is offered, not merely for the light it sheds on the possible history and development of the Gog tradition, but because it affords a good example of the form-critical methods of which Zimmerli has been such an outstanding exponent, and which have been so fruitful in what I have called 'phase three' of Ezekiel criticism.

Some of the most important techniques to note are: (1) the reliance on introductory (and ending) formulae as markers for where units begin and end; (2) the use of other form-critical criteria for designating the sense units, for instance the recognition of the 'proof-saying'; (3) the recognition of amplificatory additions, through comparison with the versions, through examination of the content (for example in 38.17-19, which is ostensibly addressed to the birds, whereas vv. 21-29 are not, in fact, so addressed), through changes in address or person (for example at 38.18 where a prophecy addressed to Gog in the second person suddenly switches to talking *about* him in the third person).

The whole of the Gog passage is introduced by a 'messenger formula', 'The word of the Lord came to me' (38.1). This is undated. The Gog tradition is not, therefore, part of the dated series of materials which we have examined elsewhere. Does this suggest (this is my suggestion, not Zimmerli's) that the Gog materials are not part of the 'hard core' from which the book developed?

Zimmerli analyses the structure of chs. 38–39 and finds it to fall into four major units, each introduced by a slightly different formula:

1. 38.2-13: 'Son of Man, set your face towards Gog...'
2. 38.14-23: 'therefore, Son of Man, prophesy and say to Gog...'
3. 39.1-16: 'And you, Son of Man, prophesy against Gog...'
4. 39.17-29: 'As for you, Son of Man, thus says Yahweh God, "Speak to the birds..." '

In units 1-3 God himself is addressed. Unit 4 (according to its introduction) is addressed to the birds and wild animals. Zimmerli decides to analyse unit 4 first.

Analysis of Unit 4, 39.17-29

The address to the birds and animals is actually maintained only for 39.17-20, where it is ended with the formula, 'Says the Lord Yahweh'. 39.21-22 is a 'bipartite proof-saying', which *could* still be logically connected with Gog. But 39.23-29 is not connected with Gog at all. It relates to the return from exile. It ends with the proof-saying in v. 28 and is capped at the end of v. 29 with the formula 'says the Lord Yahweh'. Zimmerli concludes that the original component of this section is 39.17-20. The rest is secondary expansion. The form-critical assumption here is that the original unit is likely to have maintained the same form of address consistently throughout. The change in the address which takes place after 39.20 and the sharp change in subject matter which occurs at v. 23 justify Zimmerli in seeing 39.17-20 as the original core.

Analysis of Unit 1, 38.2-13

The unit divides into two major sections, each introduced by the same introductory formula, 'Thus says the Lord Yahweh'. This formula appears in v. 3, and again in v. 10. As far as the first section, vv. 3-9, is concerned, comparisons with the ancient translations show that the section has acquired all sorts of 'amplificatory additions' (in vv. 3-5 and 9). When these are subtracted, what remains is precisely an address to Gog.

The second section (vv. 10-13) is also addressed to Gog, but then explores his thoughts and motives in attacking Israel. Zimmerli interprets the 'colourless' introductory phrase 'on that day...', which appears in v. 10, as evidence of the secondary nature of these verses.

Analysis of Unit 2, 39.14-23

This unit is also divided into two sub-units by the messenger formula, 'Thus says the Lord Yahweh', which appears in v. 14 and again in v. 17. The parenthetical 'says the Lord Yahweh' appears in vv. 18 and 21, but this in itself does not suggest further sub-division.

There are two significant features of vv. 18-23, one relating to form and one to content. As to form, vv. 18-23 are no longer addressed to Gog, but speak *about* him in the third person. As to content, these verses ascribe to Gog and the struggle against him a cosmic significance which elsewhere in chs. 38–39 they do not possess. Considerations of form and content thus converge to prompt the conclusion that only vv. 14-16, plus 17, meet the expectations to which the introduction in v. 14a gives rise. The rest is secondary expansion. However, Zimmerli for various reasons has serious doubts even about these remaining verses and eventually decides that they are not part of the original Gog prophecy.

Analysis of Unit 3, 39.1-16

39.1-5 parallels 38.2-9. The section which comprises vv. 1-5 begins with a challenge or encounter formula and continues with the expected direct address to Gog. The formula, 'For I have spoken', is clearly meant to end the communication. In vv. 6-16 the direct address is not maintained. These verses are, moreover, not themselves a unity, being broken up by various formulae.

Zimmerli does raise the question whether vv. 9-10 (the description of Gog's weapons) and vv. 11-16 (the account of his burial) may not be the original continuation of vv. 1-5 (the announcement of his destruction), even though they are not in the form of a direct address. But he decides against this. 39.11-16, especially, has been concocted out of a painstaking concern with the purity of the land.

Zimmerli's conclusions are that 'the oldest element of the Gog pericope' is to be found in 38.1-9 (without the additions which text-critical discussion enables us to identify) together with 39.1-5 and 39.17-20. A number of other commentators have found Zimmerli's argument convincing and accept his conclusions as to the likely extent of the original core of the prophecies. Zimmerli reconstructs that original core as follows:

And the word of Yahweh came to me: Son of Man, turn your face towards Gog, the chief prince of Meshech and Tubal, and prophesy against him and say:

Thus has Yahweh said: See, I am against you, Gog, chief prince of Meshech and Tubal, and I will lead you out, [you] and all your army, horses and riders, all of them fully armed, a great company. Gomer and all his hordes, Beth Togarma, the furthest north, many nations are with you. Stand and prepare yourself, you and your whole company which have been mobilized for you, and be at my service. After a long time you will be summoned, at the end of the years you will come to a land which has been recovered from the sword, has been gathered together again from among many nations on the mountains of Israel which for long lay waste—which has been led out from among the nations, and they all dwell securely—and you will arise like the thunderstorm, will come like the cloud to cover the land.

But you, Son of Man, prophesy against Gog and say:

Thus has Yahweh said: See, I am against you, Gog, chief prince of Meshech and Tubal, and I will turn you round and will lead you by the nose and will let you come from the furthest north and will bring you to the mountains of Israel. And I will smite your bow out of your left hand and will let your arrows fall from your right hand. On the mountains of Israel you will fall, you and all your hordes and many nations who are with you. To the birds of prey, to everything that has wings, and to the wild beasts of the field I will give you as fodder. In the open field you will fall, for I have spoken [it], says Yahweh.

But you, Son of Man, thus has Yahweh said: Say to the birds,
to everything that has wings, and to all the wild beasts of the
field:
Assemble and come, gather together from round about to my
sacrifice which I will slaughter for you, a great sacrifice on
the mountains of Israel. And you shall eat flesh and drink
blood. The flesh of heroes you shall eat, and the blood of the
princes of the earth you shall drink: rams, lambs and
goats—bulls, fatlings from Bashan are they all. And you
shall eat the fat of my sacrifice which I have slaughtered for
you until you are filled and drink the blood until you are
drunk, and you shall be filled at my table with horses and
chariot horses, with heroes and all warriors, says Yahweh.

As to the date of origin of the Gog proclamation, Zimmerli
concludes that the location of the threat in the region of Asia
Minor points to a period before the rise of Persia. He therefore
thinks that the Gog theme can be traced back to the exilic
period, and conceivably even to a late phase in the preaching
of Ezekiel himself. Stylistically, Zimmerli thinks, it belongs
with the earliest stratum of the Ezekiel material, and the way
it reworks themes from earlier prophecy is characteristic of
that earliest material.

None of this answers the question as to why the Gog
prophecy is there at all. If Gog is not a historical character of
the exilic period, and if the forces ascribed to him never did
threaten Judah, why is anyone uttering prophecies against
him? Are the events here prophesied envisaged, after all, as
eschatological ones? If Zimmerli has correctly identified the
original core, we can hardly say that. The material which
most readily suggests an eschatological and cosmic interpretation of the theme is seen, on Zimmerli's analysis, as secondary. Eschatological interpretation of the Gog threat has
been placed upon the traditions, but at a stage later than that
of their origins.

A view that deserves consideration takes as its point of
departure the fact that nowhere in the book of Ezekiel, in all
the oracles against foreign nations, is there any oracle against
Babylon. This seems remarkable in view of all that Judah
suffered at Babylonian hands over the period which the book
of Ezekiel covers. It is not remarkable, however, if Ezekiel is

prophesying in Babylonia, where such oracles, if they had come to public notice, would doubtless have involved the prophet in immediate and serious trouble. What more likely, then, than that the land of Gog is a cypher for Babylon itself, and the prophecies of Gog's destruction a heavily coded message predicting the demise of the Babylonian power? This cannot, of course, be proved. If it could be proved by us, now, in the twentieth century, it could have been proved then, in the sixth, with the aforementioned unwelcome results.

This interpretation is supported by, but does not depend on, the suggestion that the name Magog is derived from the name Babel (Hebrew for Babylon), by replacing each letter of the name with the letter which precedes it in the Hebrew alphabet (hence LBB) and then turning the whole back to front, thus BaBeL. This is again an interesting but unverifiable hypothesis.

In summary, the most likely conclusion is that either the prophet himself, or someone very shortly after his time, put together a tripartite oracle, two parts being addressed to Gog and the third to the carrion birds, represented in the present text by 38.1-9, 39.1-5 and 39.17-20. Whoever did this used the name of a legendary king from what was thought of as the barbarian North. The historical original of the legend may derive from the seventh-century Gyges of Lydia. The writer modelled the work on Jeremiah's oracles about the foe from the North, and Isaiah's prophecies of the destruction of Assyria. The author of these prophecies may or may not have intended them to be understood as referring to Babylon.

These prophecies were then filled out in a multitude of stages, and at some stage or stages Gog was turned into something like an eschatological cosmic figure.

Further Reading

B.S. Childs, 'The Enemy from the North and the Chaos Tradition', *JBL* 78 (1959), pp. 187-98.
B. Otzen, 'Gogh; Maghogh', in *TDOT*, II, pp. 419-25.

INDEX OF REFERENCES

Genesis

10	117
17.20	110
18	82
19	82
23.6	111
25.16	110
34.2	111
49.10	105

Exodus

6.1-8	94
20.2	94
32.30-34	95
40.34ff.	100

Leviticus

17–19	94
19.11ff.	53
25.9	66

Numbers

3.10	88
3.38	88
4.23	23
8.24	23
13	110
15–16	88
15	88
15.32-36	88
16	87, 88
16.2	110
16.41-50	87
18.7	88
22.41	51
23.13	51
24.1-2	51

Deuteronomy

5.6	94
6.6-9	12
7.6-8	80
11.18-21	12
18.22	95
21	85
21.18-21	85, 87
24.15	84
24.16	84
32.10	97
34	102

Judges

9.7ff.	19
9.7-15	105

1 Samuel

10.6	92

1 Kings

8.10ff.	100
11.34	111
18	94
18.11-12	21
18.12	92, 93
18.46	92
20	54, 93
20.13	54, 93
20.28	54, 93
20.36	93
20.42	93
22	92, 94
22.21-24	92

2 Kings

2.11	98
2.16	21, 93

3.15	92
6.32	51
11.29ff.	20
14.9	105
24.8-17	23
24.8	72
25.8	67

Ezra

1.8	113
7.9	67

Psalms

15.1-2	53
15.2-5	53
19.11	52
24.3-4	53
24.4	53
51.10	96
81.10	94
118.19-20	53
119.103	52

Isaiah

1.13	86
1.21	96
5	19
6	13, 18
6.1	62
6.3ff.	100
7.1	62
7.3	20
7.14	20
7.20	52
8.1-4	20
8.1-2	95
8.3-4	95
8.11	51, 92

8.14-17	95	27.1	62	3.16	64, 69, 70
10.5ff.	117	27.12	50	3.17-21	56
10.12ff.	117	28.1	62	3.19	53
10.15ff.	117	28.9	95	3.22–5.17	70
10.24-27	117	29.1-32	13	3.22-27	51
14.28	62	20–31	108	3.22-24a	69, 71
20	20	30.1-2	13	3.22	21, 92
50.1	96	31	96	3.24b–5.17	70
52.13–53.12	95	31.2-3	97	3.24b–27	69
		31.29-30	95	3.24	25
Jeremiah		31.31ff.	91	3.25-27	16, 24
1.2	50, 62	31.33	96	3.25-26	28
1.11ff.	18	32.1	62	3.25	25
1.11	13	32.39	96	3.26	25
2.2-3	97	35	20	3.27	24
2.2	78	36.9	62	4–7	56
2.20-25	96	36.11	62	4–5	46, 69
2.33–3.5	96	39.1-2	67	4	20, 25, 27
3.6ff.	108	41.1	62	4.1-3	51
3.6-11	96	45.1	62	4.4-8	25, 28, 51,
3.6-10	116	49.34	62		95
3.16	12	52.4-7	67	4.8	25
4–6	116	52.7-11	77	4.9-17	28
4.11ff.	116			4.9-11	51
5.1-5	90	*Ezekiel*		4.12-15	51
5.1	83, 90	1–39	35	4.27	24
5.15-17	116	1–24	15, 38	5	20, 25, 27,
6.1ff.	116	1.1–3.15	13, 46, 48,		52
6.17	116		70	5.1ff.	28
6.22ff.	116	1	14, 18, 36,	5.1-3	51
7.9	52		71, 89	6	46
8.1-3	96	1.1ff.	16	6.11	27
9.24	94	1.1-3	23, 25	7	46, 53
11.14	82	1.1-2	64, 68	7.2	53
13.1-11	20	1.1	13, 23, 34,	7.27	111
14.1	50		63, 64, 70	8–11	16, 25, 35,
14.11	82	1.3	21, 23, 92		48, 68, 70,
15.1	82	1.4–2.2	36		99, 102
15.16	52	2.2	21	8	20, 21, 86
15.17	51, 92	2.3–3.9	36	8.1–11.13	46
16.1-4	20	2.5	16	8.1ff.	25, 51
16.5	96	3	116	8.1	21, 23, 25,
19	20	3.12	20, 21, 93		64, 68, 70,
24	90	3.14	20, 21, 92,		92
24.7	96		93	8.2-3	99
25.1	62	3.15	23	8.3	21, 41, 93
26.1	62	3.16-21	16, 69, 71,	8.6	18
27–28	20		82	8.12	18

8.15	18	16.9-14	79	21.25-27	105, 108
8.17	18	16.15-34	79	21.25	112
9–11	89	16.60-63	15	22	46, 86
9	56, 83	17	13, 19, 105, 106, 108	22.2	52
9.3-9	82, 83			22.6-12	53
9.8-10	83	17.1-10	57, 105	22.6	111
10	71	17.2	19	22.8	86
11.1	20, 21, 93	17.11-21	105	22.17-22	87
11.5	21	17.22-32	15	22.30	83
11.14-21	15, 46	17.22-24	105, 106	23–24	56
11.19	96	17.22-23	102	23	13, 19, 46,
11.20	96	17.23	106		53, 78-80,
11.22-23	16	18	12, 19, 52,		84, 96, 116
11.24	20, 21, 93,		53, 83, 84,	23.1-3	79
	99		86, 95	23.2-25	57
12	56	18.1-20	56	23.19-21	79
12.1-20	46, 69	18.5-9	53	23.32-34	13
12.1-16	20, 51, 69	18.10-13	53	23.36	52
12.3-7	28	18.23	85	23.38	86
12.10	112	18.25	52	23.39	86
12.12	112	18.29	52	24	26, 46, 70
12.17-20	20, 28, 51	19	17, 50, 56	24.1-14	16, 87
12.17	69	19.1	111	24.1	64, 68, 70
12.21–13.21	46	20	48, 70, 78-	24.3b-6	13
12.21-28	52		80, 84, 102	24.3b-5	17
12.21	69	20.1ff.	51	24.15ff.	22, 24
12.26	69	20.1	25, 64, 68,	24.15-24	20, 51
13	56, 69		70	24.16	95
13.19	87	20.4	52	24.21	86
14	46, 53, 83	20.6-8	78	24.23	107
14.1ff.	51	20.10-13	78	24.25-27	16
14.1-11	53, 56	20.14	87	24.27	24
14.1	25	20.16	86	25–32	15, 16, 38
14.2	69	20.18-21	78	25	46
14.12-20	56, 82	20.21	86	25.3-5	93
14.13	53	20.22	87	25.6-7	93
14.21-23	83	20.27-31	78	25.8-11	93
15–20	46	20.32ff.	35	25.15-17	93
15–16	56	20.33-44	81, 97	25.29	53
15.1	69	20.39	87	26–28	46
16	13, 19, 53,	21	46, 56	26	70
	78-80, 84,	21.1-16	56	26.1	64-66, 68,
	96	21.6-7	20		70
16.1	69	21.9-10	17	26.2-6	93
16.2-3	79	21.11-12	51	26.16	111
16.2	52	21.12	111	27	14
16.4-5	79	21.18-20	20	27.21	111
16.4	52	21.23-29	51	29–32	46

29.1-16	70
29.1	64, 66, 68, 70
29.6b-9a	93
29.17-21	70
29.17	63, 64, 66, 68, 70
30.1-19	70
30.13	111
30.20-26	71
30.20	64, 66, 71
31	71
31.1	64, 66, 71
32	36
32.1-16	71
32.1	64-66, 71
32.17-32	71
32.17	64-67, 71
32.29	111
33–48	15, 33
33–39	38
33	36, 46, 69, 71, 82, 116
33.1-20	56
33.1-9	16
33.2	53
33.6	53
33.9	53
33.10ff.	52
33.15	53
33.21-22	16, 24, 28, 50, 66, 71
33.21	23, 64, 67, 71
33.22	92
33.30-31	25
33.31	51
33.33	16
34	19, 46, 85, 106, 108
34.9-10	106
34.11-16	106
34.14	102
34.17-19	106, 107
34.20-22	106
34.23-24	106, 107
34.24	111, 112
35	15, 46
35.5-9	93
36–39	46
36	26
36.16-32	35
36.20	87
36.21	87
36.22	87
36.23	87
36.24-25	28
36.26-27	96
36.28	96
37	12, 14, 16, 18, 26, 96, 107, 108, 114
37.1ff.	25
37.1	20, 21, 92
37.11-14	35, 52, 107
37.15-28	51, 107
37.15-23	20
37.15-19	107
37.20-23	107
37.24-28	107
37.25	108, 111, 112
38–39	31, 38, 39, 114-22
38.1-9	120, 122
38.1-5	119, 122
38.1	117
38.2-13	118
38.2-9	119
38.2	111
38.3-9	118
38.3-5	118
38.3	111, 118
38.5	116
38.9	118
38.10-13	119
38.10	118, 119
38.14-23	118
38.17-19	117
38.18	117
38.21-29	117
39.1-16	119
39.1-5	119, 120, 122
39.1	111
39.6-16	119
39.9-10	119
39.11-16	119, 120
39.14-23	119
39.14-16	119
39.14	119
39.17-29	118
39.17-20	118, 120, 122
39.17	119
39.18-23	119
39.18	111, 119
39.20	118
39.21-22	118
39.21	119
39.23-29	118
39.23	118
39.28	118
39.29	118
40–48	18, 31, 38, 46, 48, 71, 89, 99-104
40.1ff.	25
40.1-4	100
40.1-2	20, 99
40.1	21, 23, 36, 63-66, 71, 92
40.2	102
40.6–42.20	100, 101
43.1ff.	16
43.1-12	100
43.1-5	89, 102
43.5	21, 93
43.13-27	100
44.1-3	100, 101
44.3	112
44.4-27	100
44.5-31	101
44.7	86
44.28-31	100
45.1-9	100, 101
45.7-8	101
45.7	112
45.8-9	111
45.10–46.15	101
45.10-17	100
45.13–46.18	102

45.16	112	*Daniel*		8.1ff.	18
45.17	112	4.10-12	106	8.2	53
45.18-25	100	4.20-22	106	9.1ff.	18
45.22	112			9.1	13
46.1-15	100	*Hosea*			
46.2	112	1	13	*Micah*	
46.4	112	1.2-9	20	3.8	92
46.8	112	2.14-15	78, 97		
46.10	112	3	13	*Haggai*	
46.12	112	4.1	52	2.10-14	97
46.16-18	100	9.7	92		
46.16	112	9.10	97	*Zechariah*	
46.17	112	10.11	97	1.7–6.8	19, 97
46.18	112				
46.19-24	100, 101	*Amos*		*Malachi*	
47.1-12	100	3.12	83	1.6–2.16	98
47.13-20	100, 101	4.6-12	90		
47.21–48.29	101	7.1-9	18	*1 Enoch*	
48.21-22	101, 112	7.8	13	17–36	98
48.30-35	101	7.10-17	95		

INDEX OF AUTHORS

Albright, W.F. 115
Ackroyd, P.R. 91
Allen, E.L. 9
Auvray, P. 36

Bertholet, A. 36, 37
Bettenzoli, G. 56
Boadt, L. 10
Broome, E. 29
Browne, L.E. 38, 115
Brownlee, W.H. 10
Bruce, F.F. 10
Budde, K. 33

Carley, K.W. 9, 92-95, 98
Cassuto, U. 21
Childs, B.S. 21, 59-61, 122
Clements, R.E. 54, 55, 61
Cooke, G.A. 9, 37
Corrodi, H. 31

Davis, E.F. 24, 61
Driver, S.R. 30, 31, 41

Duhm, B. 33
Dürr, L. 115

Eichrodt, W. 9, 24, 67, 77
Eissfeldt, O. 27, 43, 48, 49, 61, 72

Finegan, J. 72
Fisch, S. 9
Fishbane, M. 21
Fohrer, G. 26, 43-48, 57, 61

Garscha, J. 56-58, 61
Gese, H. 97, 103, 104
Graf Reventlow, H. 61
Greenberg, M. 9, 46, 47, 58-61
Gressmann, P. 115

Heinisch, P. 115
Herntrich, V. 35-37
Herrmann, J. 33
Herrmann, S. 39
Hölscher, G. 33-35, 41

Ezekiel

Hossfeld, F.L. 56, 58, 61
Howie, C.G. 29, 38

Irwin, W.A. 42

Jaspers, K. 29
Joyce, P. 75, 82, 84, 85, 91
Koch, K. 91
Kraetzschmar, R. 32, 33, 35
Krüger, T. 91
Kutsch, E. 67

Levenson, J.D. 91, 104
Lindars, B. 91
Lindholm, J. 29, 91
Lust, J. 61

Matthews, I.G. 36
May, H.G. 9
Messel, N. 37, 115
Moran, W.L. 105, 109
Muilenberg, J. 10
Mullo-Weir, C.J. 38, 42

Oeder, G.L. 31
Otzen, B. 122
Pfeiffer, R.H. 38-40, 42

Rad, G. von 91, 93

Rendtorff, R. 21, 27, 50, 57
Robinson, H.W. 36, 42

Rowley, H.H. 42

Schmidt, W.H. 21
Schultz, H. 56-58
Seinecke, L. 31
Simian, H. 56
Smend, R. 31
Smith, J. 35
Spiegel, S. 36
Stalker, D.M. 9

Talmon, S. 21
Taylor, J.B. 9
Torrey, C.C. 34, 35, 42, 115

Van den Born, A. 36, 38, 115

Weiser, A. 47, 48, 57, 61

Wevers, J.W. 10
Widengren, G. 29
Wilson, R.R. 10, 29

Zimmerli, W. 10, 19, 25, 43, 49-55,
    57-62, 91, 93, 98, 108, 112, 113,
    117-21
Zunz, L. 31